50+ Marketing

50+ MARKETING

Marketing, communicating and selling to the over 50s generations

Jean-Paul Tréguer

palgrave

Published 2002 by
PALGRAVE
Houndmills, Basingstoke, Hampshire RG21 6XS and
175 Fifth Avenue, New York, N.Y. 10010
Companies and representatives throughout the world

PALGRAVE is the new global academic imprint of
St. Martin's Press LLC Scholarly and Reference Division and
Palgrave Publishers Ltd (formerly Macmillan Press Ltd).

ISBN 0–333–98412–9 hardcover

This book is printed on paper suitable for recycling and
made from fully managed and sustained forest sources.

A catalogue record for this book is available
from the British Library.

A catalogue record for this book is available
from the Library of Congress.

Editing and origination by
Aardvark Editorial, Mendham, Suffolk

10 9 8 7 6 5 4 3 2 1
11 10 09 08 07 06 05 04 03 02

Printed and bound in Great Britain by
Creative Print & Design (Wales), Ebbw Vale

Contents

LIST OF FIGURES AND TABLES

Figures

Tables

About the Author

Jean-Paul Tréguer is French, a child of the baby-boom era, and holds a business diploma (EDHEC). He has three children, Arnaud, Amaury and Alicia.

After a career spent with several international advertising agencies, he became founding president of *Senioragency*, the first and only independent advertising specialist network for baby boomers and the over 50s (located in Paris, London, Tokyo, Brussels, Amsterdam, Vienna and Oslo) that is developing on a franchise basis.

He is the first European professional specialist in generational marketing and since 1989 has devoted himself exclusively to this field that is so poorly understood by other publicists and agencies. He and his team have advised numerous US, European and Japanese companies, on strategic matters, training, research and development, as well as generational design, direct marketing and advertising campaigns (especially TV infomercials).

More than 100 companies have already worked with Senioragency, including the following: AXA, Coca-Cola, Danone, Essilor, LVMH, Mars, Nivea, Novartis, Johnson & Johnson, Renault, Peugeot, SCA, Siemens and the Zurich Group.

He has written several books on generational marketing to the over 50s in order to convert those working in marketing to his thinking. These include *Senior Marketing* (first French edition 1994), and *Eighteen Golden Rules for Selling to the Over 50s* (1996), which have been translated into several languages.

He is also very involved in the development of the use of the Internet by the over 50s and was co-founder in 2000 of a start-up company that has met with great success: the leading portal for the over 50s in France and Belgium (www.seniorplanet.fr).

With his excellent knowledge of English he is one of the most sought after lecturers on marketing to the over 50s, and delivers presentations at seminars and conferences for large companies throughout the four corners of the globe, as well as assisting conference organisers such as *The Economist*, IIR, Food Marketing Institute, Haymarket EFMA and Development Institute.

The Internet site www.senioragency.com has become one of the most important international forums for marketing to the over 50s. For further information contact treguer@senioragency.com.

FOREWORD

Many years ago, when I was a fledgling market researcher, I was summoned to a briefing at a very well-known food company. They had developed a range of products specially for older consumers and wanted these tested. The marketing manager proudly presented them to me. Called 'Dinners for One' they were re-labelled baby foods, each of which bore the imprint of a beaming geriatric. I was at once staggered by the ingenuity of this idea and horrified by the opportunism (but hey, that's marketing for you). Yes, it seemed to make perfectly good sense to offer a range of sweet and savoury products, the texture and taste of which would be unlikely to challenge elderly digestions, but somehow the whole thing seemed rather distasteful. Well, we tested the wretched things and I am heartily glad to tell you that, like Dr Johnson's recipe for a salad, they were 'thrown out as good for nothing'. Consumers felt patronised and rather disgusted by what they saw as a piece of naked cynicism.

I relate this tale for three reasons. First, by one of those extraordinary coincidences that can make life so enjoyable, Jean-Paul Tréguer tells *exactly* the same story in Chapter 7 and, more courageous than I, names the manufacturer (no, you must look it up yourself). Second, it was the first occasion in my so-called 'professional' career that I had encountered a new product initiative designed for elderly consumers: on reflection it was a great piece of thinking, but poorly executed. Third, it made me think that while older consumers often have different requirements from their younger counterparts, the way in which these are met by manufacturers, and the way in which they are marketed, have to be done with sensitivity.

In this book, Jean-Paul rages against the crassness of much of the marketing which targets older consumers. Such marketing is often not merely inappropriate, and sometimes downright insulting, but it misses out on what is increasingly the greatest opportunity available to businesses today: the emergence of the 'grey' market. People nowadays live longer, healthier and wealthier lives than their grandparents and, with developments in medical science and increasing affluence worldwide, future generations can look forward to a greatly enhanced quality of life. Yet in relative terms very little money is spent on the development of products and services specifically for older consumers and in advertising and promoting these. It seems that the majority of manufacturers and service companies still adhere to the Jesuitical principle of bring me the boy and I will give you the man, and concentrate their efforts on recruiting younger customers. In an age when the balance of wealth is tilting more and more towards the over 50s this seems misguided.

Why, then, are older consumers neglected in this way? This book points to a variety of reasons, many of which can be attributed to plain ignorance or superstition. Ignorance in that many commercial organisations simply fail to understand that so cohesive and powerful an economic grouping as 'the greys' really exists. Superstition in that attitudes towards older people are deeply entrenched in societies everywhere. The elderly may be venerated, but old age basically is 'uncool'. Older people are unproductive and a drain on society; they are deeply conservative in their tastes and unwilling to try new experiences. Who on earth would waste money on targeting such 'has-beens' – and what damage would this do to a company's reputation if it sought to align itself with such an unattractive target market?

Jean-Paul sets out evidence that thoroughly debunks such prejudices. He points to developments in that most enlightened of all consumer societies, the United States, and shows how the activities of powerful lobby groups, such as the American Association of Retired Persons, have led to a fundamental change in attitudes towards older consumers. Such change has entirely come about since the end of the Second World War. Perhaps it was the desire on the part of the American people genuinely to create a land 'fit for heroes to live in', coupled with a period of unprecedented affluence that helped to emancipate older people. Perhaps it was the American genius for 'spotting a buck' that helped drive the change and give shape to a powerful new economic, and political, grouping. Whatever the reason American 'seniors' enjoy a status within their society that is yet unparalleled elsewhere in the world.

Another powerful force for change has been the maturing of the 'baby boomer' generation. The youngsters who grew up in the 1960s, who rebelled, who embraced 'sex, drugs and rock 'n' roll', have come of age. Over the next ten years or so they will have retired from work – but not from life. This is the 'Peter Pan' generation that will completely redefine what old age means. Their values and beliefs, their tastes and preferences, are completely different from the present generation of over 60s. They are wealthier, better informed about health and lifestyle, and technologically more literate than their predecessors. In short, they have more options, and the power to exercise these.

Significantly, governments everywhere in the Western world are concerned about the 'economic time bomb' that is ticking away in their midst. Ageing populations place particular strains on medical and welfare services, the future viability of state pensions is in doubt, and strenuous efforts are being made to encourage far greater self-reliance in citizens and how they provide for their old age. There is a huge political and economic challenge to be faced. This, perhaps above all else, will help to bring the 'senior agenda' to the fore and clarify the almost limitless opportunities that will arise for enterprises to compete for, and win the hearts and minds of, a hugely powerful section of the population. This book deals in plain terms with these opportunities; and companies and organisations that still believe that securing a franchise amongst youth will guarantee a business for life will find nought for their comfort here.

TOM BLACKETT
Group Deputy Chairman, Interbrand

PREFACE

I had the good fortune to 'come under the spell' of marketing to the over 50s in 1989 during one of my trips to New York. At the time I never thought that this chance meeting with a director of the all-powerful association of US pensioners, the famous AARP that boasts 32 million members, would completely alter my professional career. I was then an 'ordinary' French advertising executive, that is to say a person deeply convinced of the relevance of the under 50s households as the preferred target for all effective advertising. All my marketing expertise was focused on their behaviour and expectations and on those of their children who had to be won over from a young age in order to build the future for the brands. But, on that day, for the first time in my career, an American explained to me how current and future marketing lay much more with the over 50s than with younger generations, whose numbers were very rapidly going to be swamped by the tidal wave of the over 50s. He ended his remarks with a typical American comment that would forestall any hesitation by saying 'the over 50s – that's where the money is!'

For my part, I had never heard anyone speak of them. Nevertheless, on my return to Europe I enthusiastically began to study this new breed of consumer that was beginning to emerge, an enthusiasm that eventually led me to write two books on the subject: *Le Senior Marketing* in 1994, and *Les 18 règles d'or pour séduire les Seniors* in 1996.

For three years, I was content to study this group from all angles in France, Europe and the USA. In 1992, I felt ready to talk about it and to advise companies by creating the first European observatory for the over 50s target market. I was especially fortunate in convincing the international management of Beiersdorf-Nivea in Hamburg, Germany of the growing importance of this sector of the population and assisted them for several years, during which the Nivea Vital range was launched. This was to provide a marketing electric shock to many advertisers in every sector. It confirmed that it was possible to create specific products for the over 50s and run advertising campaigns that stated this clearly without causing any damage to the brand.

In 1995, I took the decision to devote myself completely to this market of the future by launching the first international agency dedicated exclusively to the over 50s market. Under the name Senioragency it has developed very rapidly at an international level, thanks to the demand from companies and the lack of knowledge and interest in this target market on the part of generalist advertising agencies.

Has the general panorama of marketing and advertising changed much since March 1994, when the first edition of *Senior Marketing* was published? At the risk of appearing a pessimist, I would say not.

The key concept of marketing is more or less intact. The sacrosanct target, the under 50-year-old household purchaser, remains dominant and all media plans in the large developed countries and even in developing countries continue to be drawn up with this in view. As soon as one of the media contains an increasing proportion of over 50s, advertising investment collapses and the commercial teams of the media go back to their arguments in favour of their viewers, listeners and readers in the 18–34 or 35–49 age groups.

Wherever you go in the world, you will see the same phenomenon. The over 50s make up an increasingly important sector of the population (often more than 30%) and they possess a purchasing power vastly superior to the under 50 generations (generally in the region of 40% to 45% of the national purchasing power). They increasingly consume everything (their market share of the hundreds of consumer, equipment and services markets is often greater than 40%), and yet 95% of marketing and advertising investment continues to be aimed at the under 50s! Less than 5% is devoted to this enormous potential. There is a worrying level of overt ageism in marketing and advertising. We will quote two comments made by practitioners in the media and space-buying world that are perfect illustrations of this indifference.

> They are the target group who have money, but at the same time they have everything. They are therefore not very active consumers. (Ann Strömberg, CIA, Expressen, March 2001)

> We don't forbid pensioners to watch our programmes, but there is no money to be made from letting them do so. (Staffan Erfor, TV, Expressen, March 2001)

A controversy that is all the rage and which causes me to be attacked regularly on TV talk shows revolves around the buying power of the retired. Once again, some attempt to portray 50+ marketing as a ploy to steal money from the old and feeble and drive them to over-consumption when a good number of them live in a precarious financial state. It is important to be precise about this and put a few facts in place. There is no question of claiming that all over 50s are rich; this would be failing to recognise that in many countries retired people (especially widows) live in very difficult financial conditions. Nevertheless, the facts are obstinate and it can no longer be argued that globally the over 50s are in a much better financial position than those under 50. What gives much more cause for concern today is the lowering of living standards of the younger generations who are driven by a labour market that does not open up for them. In its annual report for 1997 the French Council for Employment, Revenues and Costs stressed the increasing difference in standard of living between the young households (aged 25–29), and the older households (aged 50–59); in 1970 the average was 10%, rising to 20–30% in 1989 and reaching 30–40% in 1994.

I would even claim that the over 50s have an essential role in consumption. If they, who have the purchasing power, do not consume, how will our businesses be able to create jobs? The purpose of 50+ marketing is precisely to help companies to identify the specific needs and expectations of this clientele in order to satisfy it better and stimulate it to acquire the goods and services, all in the general interests of the economy. As Robert Rochefort, the well known French specialist in consumer behaviour, stated in the conclusion of the CREDOC study of March 1997 devoted to the power and economic role of the over 50s:

> Today 64% of the over 50s believe that advertising is not intended for them but for the young. And suppose this was why the advertising sector was in crisis? And suppose this was why it was necessary to continue to make the whole of society sensitive to the economic power of the over 50s?

Let us also quote a British expert, Roger Coleman, director of Design Age at the Royal College of Art.

> My own view is that the wrong messages are being sent out to older people. They are offered the wrong things, in the wrong way, and in the wrong context. Negative social attitudes are reinforced in subtle and unintended ways and the customer offer as a whole is inappropriate. As a consequence, older people vote with their feet, hang on to their money, or spend it on holidays and outings that offer pleasure and companionship.

There are also those who proclaim loudly and strongly that although it might be intuitively sound to take an interest in the over 50s, when one considers the threats to funding of pensions and the new tax deductions brought in by successive governments, the 'golden age' of the over 50s will never arrive and 50+ marketing is a false trail. Once again, in response to all those who abandon the economic target of the over 50s in this way we should refer them to all the statistical projections which show that the financial and patrimonial domination of the over 50s has only just begun and will increase at least threefold over the next 15 years. This is for the following reasons:

1. Large numbers of women over 50 will reach pensionable age bringing two pensions to the household instead of one (in fact the baby-boom generation will have been the first in Western society to have enjoyed a two-salary working life).

2. The pensions payable in the next 15 years will be higher, in spite of the tax deductions, because the salaries of these persons will have been higher during their careers than those of the current pensioners.

3. They have built up their estate in a period when the credit rate was very favourable and will in future years inherit substantial sums from parents who belong to a very thrifty and materially-minded generation.

At this point it is time to remind everyone that, even if the over 50s did not have so much money, it remains true that the ageing process brings into play spectacular physical and psychological developments which necessitate the adaptation of products, services, the daily environment and methods of communication in order to appeal to a generation whose 'centre of gravity' has altered. Design for the over 50s will become as essential as 50+ marketing in order to avoid the risk of the massive 'ghetto-isation' of a major sector of the population being made uncomfortable or at risk from a range of products, packaging, methods of transport both individual and public and environments conceived by the young for the young. Our American friends are certainly in advance of us in this area. In the USA, the over 50s are used systematically as the pilot target for ergonomic research, such as pens for arthritic hands that are found everywhere, easily opened medicine containers, or redesigned hotel accommodation for older people. Former President Bill Clinton reminded many of our contemporaries of the physical changes linked to the ageing process when he announced in the middle of 1997 that he was suffering from incipient deafness and that in his 52nd year he had had to equip himself with hearing aids.

Have there been any movements or initiatives to allow one to believe that things have progressed since 1994?

Unquestionably, the thesis that the over 50s are a real market has become a recurrent theme in the print and audiovisual media. One has given up trying to keep track of the international conferences or seminars devoted to them and the number of memoranda or end of study reports that discuss different aspects of the ageing of the population are countless. This permanent activity helps to convince companies of the major opportunity that the over 50s offer. Brand managers are becoming increasingly aware of the declining effectiveness of the marketing generalist who claims to win over, with the same advertising message, consumers as unbelievably disparate as young people that have not yet started work, mothers of young families and over 50s who have a whole lifetime's experience of consumption behind them. The alternative offered by generational marketing is beginning to be listened to more attentively and less condescendingly. It must be admitted that we are assisted in this by information from the USA where marketing is segmented more and more into ethnic marketing – marketing for Hispanics, for African Americans, for affluent Americans, for generation X; also, gay advertising and the latest fashionable approach, one-to-one marketing which pushes marketing segmentation to its limits. Virtually no American business now bases its development strategy on massive campaigns across all the media. They adopt an encirclement strategy sending specific messages to different targets and emphasising particular products or services using different media according to the preferences of the different consumer groups.

Why are the theories of generational marketing, invented in 1968 in the USA by Daniel Yankelovich, now finally gaining ground in Europe and elsewhere?

The answer is quite simply because it is common-sense marketing. Who would dare to suggest that in order to win over an adolescent it is not essential to know his benchmark values, his language, his heroes and his music? Who would dare suggest that a general message intended for all consumers would be more effective than a generational message?

This is why 50+ marketing is gaining converts, quite simply because it is more effective. Since publication of the first edition of the book *le senior marketing* several advertising campaigns have shown certain companies how this target market could react very positively if it was approached with delicacy and relevance. Some of these are McDonald's in the USA, Zuritel with Eric Tabarly in France and Nivea Vital with the beautiful Suzanne Schöneborn in Europe. To these we should add the magnificent campaign run by the Unilever Group for its Olivio brand in Europe and the New Zealand milk collective's 'Milk Legendary Stuff' that featured a handsome retired milkman continuing to ply his trade, in his own style, with his former housewife customers.

Another factor to note is the shouting from more and more commentators who are exasperated by the ostracism of the over 50s. An example is Bernard Pivot, the well-known French literary journalist and commentator, who wrote the following in his book *Reproof to the households of the under 50s* (Plon), published in February 1998:

> It remains to be seen if, at the age of 50, you are as unfashionable and disconnected from life as advertisers and publicists suggest. Of course not, and their blindness is stupefying. Only experts in marketing have never come across terribly careful 50-year-olds pushing trolleys that groan under the weight of their purchases in supermarket car parks.

To end this introduction I would like to quote Tom Peters who said:

> The end of the 1990s favours the culture of speed. There will only be two types of manager: the speedy and the dead!

If after reading this book you are convinced of the extraordinary potential of the over 50s, do not hesitate to act. Just do it.

ACKNOWLEDGEMENTS

My thanks to all my friends and colleagues around the world who, through their various contributions, have enabled me to write this new book by drawing on their knowledge of the over 50s. I hope that the result will add something to the fund of knowledge about the behaviour, needs and aspirations of the mature generations.

First, I should like to thank the team of '50+ marketing evangelists', who spread the good word about *Senioragency* around the globe. They are, first and foremost, Jean-Marc Segati; then Thierry Hermant, Edgar Keehnen, Ole Werring, Hans Christensen, Neil Jenner, Peter Schilling, Yuko Wada, Terruo Haga; then the 'generation' team of Bipe – Bernard Préel and Pascale Hebel; and finally, my friend at AARP, Hal Norvell, for his enlightened knowledge of the American over 50s.

I should also like to thank the team of our Internet portal *Seniorplanet* and the following for their advice and vital contributions: Patrice Angot, Christian Alexandre, Joël Binet, Nicolas Birouste, Tom Blackett, Pierre Boulet, Eric Bousquet, Katy Brulant, Marie Laure Cahier, Benjamin Cassan, Thierry Casseville, Pascal Cirotteau, Christiane Collange, Benjamin Courty, Yann Dacquay, Jean-Luc Excousseau, Françoise Forette, Guena, David Genzel, Hugues de Jouvenel, Didier Leduc, Babeth Leforissier, Olivier Lefriec, Bernard Maître, Rachel Maquin, Arnaud Marcilhacy, Isabelle Monanimo, Gilles Perony, Claire Verqualie, Isabelle Vaurs, Chahan Kazandjian, Christian de Perthuis, Mihanta Rabefitseheno, Rodolphe Roux, Jean-Yves Ruault, Stephen Rutt, Malcolm Stewart my translator, Philippe Tissandier, Elisabeth Veistroffer. My warmest thanks and admiration go to Xavier Fontanet, Rolf Kunisch, Lars Olofsson and Peter M. Thompson who read and reviewed this book.

Last, but not least, I again wish to express my gratitude and pride that Tom Blackett, Group Deputy Chairman of Interbrand, has provided the Foreword. I do not forget that it is thanks to him that this book is published.

CHAPTER 1

An incredible marketing blindspot

There's none so blind as they that won't see
JONATHAN SWIFT

If there is one statistical domain that is easy to project into the future it is demography. Here there is no need for futurologist, magicians or card readers to tell us about tomorrow. We just have to follow the curves and within a few per cent they can show us what the demographic structure of a country will be in 10, 15 or 20 years. Such information is readily available and fully annotated in the latest census reports from national and international demographic institutions. What is more, this information is free.

In an economic world in which every year billions of dollars and euros are spent on consumer studies, panels, test-marketing, pre-tests and post-tests, in order to better understand the attitudes and behaviour of consumers faced with products and services from competing companies, and with studies that are jealously scrutinised and analysed by cohorts of eminent directors (research, marketing, strategy, communication, media, and so on), how can it be that the most important demographic phenomenon of the beginning of this new century has passed by virtually unnoticed?

The planet is ageing. Our continent more than ever now deserves its name Old Europe. The USA and Japan are struck by the same phenomenon and almost no one seems to see it, or draw the obvious marketing and communication conclusions from it. Even today, nearly 95% of the media plans drawn up by advertisers and agencies are aimed at the sacrosanct under 50s buyers because, as everyone knows, after 50 one no longer consumes or spends, perhaps because one is dead? A perfect illustration of one-idea marketing!

The study of the mass media (such as TV or the press) is interesting because they are the mirror of our society and they reflect the dominant culture of a given period. In 1998, six European public service broadcast organisations joined forces in the Gender Portrayal Network: YLE (Finland), NOS (the Netherlands), SVT (Sweden), NRK (Norway) and ZDF (Germany). The basic database for this study comprises 371 hours of prime time TV and 10,497 speaking individuals. Regarding age, it can be concluded that people over 65 hardly figure in prime time TV; only 2% of the people seen in prime time were aged 65+. In this age group, twice as many men, compared with women, were presented. There were scarcely any differences between the six countries. A total of 7423 minutes of speaking time was analysed, showing that people over 65 accounted for 239 minutes (3%) in total! In prime time TV, only 2% of the leading actors were over 65 and they were all male (from the study, 'Who speaks in television', November 1998).

We will quote from another research study, 'Older people on television', conducted by the BBC and Age Concern in the UK in March 1998. Researchers watched 356 programmes lasting 168 hours on the following British channels: BBC1, BBC2, ITV, Channel 4, Channel 5, UK Gold and Sky One. Despite the fact that people aged 60+ represent 20% of the UK population and watch an average of 35 hours of TV per week (more than any other group), the research showed that only 10% of presenters, reporters, interviewees, contestants and fictional characters were over 60. Compared with younger people, older people had less prominent roles on television: 96% of older people were interviewees, compared with only 76% of younger people; 3% of older people were major presenters compared with 9% of younger people; and 1% of older people were minor presenters compared with 15% of younger people.

To conclude this research overview established by the Dutch media researcher, Huub Evers, working for NPOE (the Netherlands Platform for Older People and Europe), we will consider the Dutch study (van Selm, Westerhof and Thissen) made in 1996 on images of older people (50+) in commercials; this involved a content analysis of some 1000 commercials. Older adults were shown in only 3% of these (that is, 28 commercials).

Elderly persons, and especially older women, appeared to be highly under-represented. Above all, older people appear in commercials in which food, especially sweets, is recommended. Also, a high proportion of the commercials deal with financial issues, such as pensions and insurance. Generally, older people play a characteristic role and they are not the target group. Only a few commercials (for example, those concerning health support products, such as reading-glasses and incontinence towels) are aimed at older adults as a target group. A considerable number of commercials (60%) were humorous. The authors interpret the results as characteristic of a predominantly negative portrayal of older people.

How are we to explain why so many experts in marketing and communication, whose talent and professionalism cannot be doubted, uniformly neglect millions of moneyed and available consumers who have only to be wooed?

The key to this mystery may be found in the following seven points.

A panicky fear of death

We have a fear of dying and anything that reminds us of this event makes us profoundly uneasy.

In the West our relationship with death is considerably affected by the strength of the dominant religions. In India, for example, the attitude towards death is infinitely less tense and dramatic, since it is seen as a necessary step towards reincarnation. Any tourist visiting the Indian subcontinent is amazed at the nonchalance of the thousands of pedestrians squatting at the roadside who remain where they are even when they are brushed by lorries passing at full speed. Culturally, death is not perceived as an end, but as a new departure. In the West, the reaction is different; we are tortured by the prospect of death and we therefore blot out this unattractive image (the 'ostrich' policy).

Old age is perceived as the antechamber of death. When we see old people (and as we know the concept of 'old' is always relative: a man of 25 will be very old for a child of 10, and an adult of 50 will appear old to a young graduate fresh from college), we immediately ascribe to them all the attributes of old age: illness, peevish character, disabilities, dependency, incontinency and so on. Preconceived ideas about the over 50s are countless and their importance in the minds of the public is, as we shall see, considerable.

The loss of status of the elderly

In the history of the majority of civilisations, the elders have played, and in many continents continue to play, the role of wise men and women who are consulted when decisions about the community have to be taken. This is a natural and uncontested role, since nothing can replace experience when it comes to decision-making.

On the professional front, there can be little doubt that it takes tens of years of practice, with success and failure, in order to perfect one's trade or skill. In the Middle Ages, the apprenticeship among the cathedral builders bears witness to this requirement. In Japan, where the cult of the elder has long been one of the essential pillars of society, these people are called 'living treasures'. The whole population venerates them because they are trustees of an ancestral knowledge in the highly esteemed domains of Japanese culture and art; lacquer work, engraving, indigo dyeing and metalwork. In the world of art, writing and music, the art never ceases to develop and expand with the passing of time.

However, in our Western societies the role of the elder has continued to diminish for decades to the point where all authority has been lost. Within the family cell, the grandparents no longer live with their children and grandchildren (accommodation too inadequate, professional migration, desire for independence, and so on). Within the company, the combined pressures of economic crisis and rising unemployment drive directors to push thousands of experienced staff into early retirement because in their eyes they have two major defects: they are older and more expensive to employ that younger staff.

We will quote the comment by Maximilienne Levet and Chantal Pelletier in their French book, *Le Papy Boom*, on the connotations of the word 'old':

> The word old is used a lot in French. It has magic powers and can on its own transform a banal word into an insult: old buffer, old fogy, old picture. When put before an insult it simply turns it into a superlative: it is less humiliating to be called an idiot than an old idiot.

Our society dreams of a world where the young hold power at a time when all the statistics show the futility of such a dream.

The dictatorship of youth, beauty and activity

The myth of youth is a collective obsession that dominates our cultural, economic and political life. Looking young is the guiding order of the day.

This obsession sometimes borders on the ridiculous when some political figures, in order to appeal to the younger electorate, take to using what they believe to be the language of adolescents. Such behaviour, which is

so widespread to be anecdotal, has led the psychiatrist Yves Pélicier to
come up with the following analysis:

> In some primitive societies, eating a young animal, drinking the blood of a
> young creature or having sex with a very young person was said to have reju-
> venating qualities. Today, we are witnessing a modern version of this sacred
> cannibalism. The youth culture is like a magic cult.

Is growing old a shameful thing? Yes, if we are to believe the leaders of
mass communication.

This is why the men and women in the posters, on magazine covers and
in the TV sitcoms are so handsome and attractive.

They have been there since the 1960s and don't have a wrinkle! Still
slim, sun-tanned and sexy, increasingly unclothed, with exotic or seductive
expressions. They are all different but all share a common facet: they are
bursting with youth. (And do they not say that the career of a model is
over when she is 25?)

This idealised view of the body and beauty allows for few exceptions.
Advertisers have interiorised this ideal of women and men to such a point
that it is very rare for them to use an older model. When one is used, it is
generally in an exaggerated context.

We are therefore now in a century where more than 30% of the population of developed countries is 50 or older and where the vast majority of
advertising campaigns continue to portray male and female consumers as
though there had been no demographic evolution. To quote Nick Long of
Market Behaviour Ltd:

> Advertising executives, mostly under 30, were profoundly uninterested in
> understanding the over 50s and their views and associations were largely with
> stereotypes of decrepitude, imbecility and physical repugnance.

One of the primordial functions of an advertising campaign is to trigger
identification of the projected model. Can we really hope that millions of
consumers will recognise themselves in the young people who might just
as well be their children, or their grandchildren?

Mistaken identity

The test is striking. Ask people point-blank: 'Describe a retired man to
me.' You will then be given in large measure a portrait worthy of the nine-

teenth century. 'He is not very rich, not very healthy, holds reactionary political views, lives buried in his small suburban house, from where he only ventures in his cloth cap to collect his pension and his daily paper. Back home he might listen to some Glenn Miller or Ella Fitzgerald before blissfully settling down in front of his TV where he will swallow all the rubbish before falling asleep in his chair every evening.'

Faced with this question, the natural tendency for most people is to describe the popular view of society portrayed in films and novels since the end of the Second World War. It is also an unconscious portrayal of the lifestyle of our grandparents. This generation was the disadvantaged of the twentieth century. Born before the First World War, they subsequently experienced all kinds of fear and privation that marked them for life. They emerged with their health often weakened and a morbid fear of failing. With such images in our heads, we often forget that an early retired person, may well only be 57 or 58, enjoy good physical health, be cultivated and interested in everything, possess more than adequate available income and enjoy rock music as he has done all his life (one has only to recall audience shots at concerts by the Rolling Stones, Pink Floyd or Phil Collins).

Advertising and marketing: the youth tribe

How powerful is the microcosm? In Paris, New York, London and Tokyo, some thousands of individuals look after on the one hand the marketing (the advertisers), and on the other the communication (the agencies). They rule over thousands of brands which every year spend tens of billions of dollars and euros on advertising campaigns. This is the tribe of marketing and advertising executives.

Like all tribes, they have the same origins, the same thought patterns, the same benchmarks, the same haunts. They have graduated from a large commercial college or university. They admire the rigour of Procter & Gamble, Nestlé, Danone and Colgate, and the creativity of L'Oréal or Pepsi.

They would never fail to read the latest issue of their professional press (*Advertising Age*, *Campaign*, *Stratégies*, and so on) while at the same time pretending to take a very detached view of such publications. They frequent the same fashionable restaurants, the same film previews and subscribe to the same sports clubs. They never fail to attend the 'high mass' of their profession, namely the Cannes Festival of Advertising Film.

Above all, they share one special characteristic: they are overwhelmingly young. With an average age of 28 to 35, marketing directors and group heads of marketing communicate easily with agency executives and creative staff, where it is a well-known fact that, after 45, if one has not become the chairman one is no longer working in advertising. For example, in the UK, the Institute of Practitioners in Advertising revealed that of the 12,800 people working in its member agencies in 2000, only 776 were aged over 50. In the USA, it has been shown that 82% of people working in advertising agencies were under 40, while 39% of the marketing directors were under 35 and only 10% over 50.

Should we regret this youth? Certainly not, since it is partly what enables advertisers and agencies to come up constantly with the new products and new ideas that constitute the dynamic of this industry.

Nonetheless, it is also one of the basic reasons that explain this unbelievable 'marketing genocide' of millions of over 50-year-olds.

Living in this half enclosed world, the advertiser and his agent naturally find it difficult to establish contact with a consumer who is two or three times their age. It is much more convenient to communicate with people of one's own generation whose reactions and expectations are more easily anticipated and understood.

In conclusion, we should recognise that the baby boom (1946–64) and the socio-economic context created a euphoric economy that has facilitated the sale of goods and services of all kinds. The younger generations did not hesitate to buy the latest products, taking full advantage of the credit facilities offered by every store department. These cohorts of avid consumers created the good times for advertisers during this amazing development of the consumer society.

Today's scene is quite different and the over 50s could well be the lifebuoy for many markets.

The age of the captains

We should not apportion all blame for the marketing blindness to the advertising and agency executives. There is another factor that plays its part: the age of the company directors.

How many times have I observed at the end of countless strategic seminars presented to company boards the half joking, half serious response of the chairman and directors, all generally in their 50s.

They had just become aware that they belonged to this age group and for those of them who were particularly concerned about their projected image, this came as a shock. It is well known that 50-year-olds are especially shy about their age (except when they can benefit from a special service or tariff).

People do not like to see themselves growing old and, consciously or unconsciously, that markedly affects their attitude towards the strategic choices in their business. At heart, the dream of many directors is to be like Richard Branson, the emblematic head of Virgin, experienced businessman, in his 50s, but a perpetual instigator and innovator who shows himself to be younger than many who are actually younger than him. It is somewhat the myth of the boss who is forever up-to-date with the trends that is involved when one shows that the over 50s have specific needs and values that require dedicated generational marketing.

The fear of giving an 'oldie' image to one's business

'For years, I have done everything to promote my brand with the best – a young image, a young target group, a young advertising style, and you want me to take the risk of tarnishing it by appealing to the over 50s?' That is the near instinctive reaction of advertisers when the 50+ market comes up for discussion. But, in the American market, brands popular with teenagers, such as Levi's, McDonald's, Coca-Cola, Nike, Kellogg's or Pepsi, have shown for several years that these approaches are not irreconcilable.

Nevertheless, it is clear that for a very large number of companies this argument is a strong brake on the emergence of marketing strategies that include the 50+ group. This reticence comes from a tendency to caricature the strategies employed to include the over 50s in the marketing approach. But things are not simply black or white. There is no de facto reason why the integration of the over 50s into the design of products or into the communication strategy should cause the loss of the younger market.

We can even claim that, in many cases, the values produced, such as ease of use, or the communication values, such as greater rapprochement between generations, are able to bring spectacular success in both the younger and older groups. A French study, carried out in July 1997 by IED (the Youth Institute), involving 400 young people aged 18–25, corroborates this claim. In response to the question: 'More and more companies are offering products and services and advertising campaigns aimed at people aged from 50 to 70. What do you think of this?', the replies were as follows: 'I think it is quite normal for the brands to be interested in the over 50s' (36%); 'I think that these brands become more attractive by taking an interest in all generations' (27%); 'It makes no difference to me; it's not important' (32%); 'I find it makes the brands look old' (only 2%).

On the other hand, portraying over 50s in an unfavourable or confrontational light in order to appeal to the young runs the serious risk of displeasing everyone. For a number of years advertisers have been in the habit of using laughable 50+ people to show younger generations that their brands ran no risk of being consumed by such grotesque beings. Every year, throughout the world, there are new campaigns for products aimed at the young that use over the 50s as a contrast foil. This provokes much amusement among a few hundred advertising executives who take the opportunity of awarding themselves prizes for such work, but the commercial outcome is generally disastrous. This is because it is persistently forgotten that the over 50s are also buyers and within the family group there is little conflict between the generations; the grandchildren love their grandparents and do not see them at all in the way that the advertisers depict them.

What interest do companies have in making enemies of millions of consumers, shocked and even offended by the negative representation of their generation? Humour is fine, but why this type? As Hege Christensen and Kristin Undheim, authors of the *Bengal Trend Report on Scandinavian Seniors* (July, 2000), write:

> Seniors are the mass media's most faithful customers, but neither advertisers nor TV companies are particularly interested by them. They don't think that they will able to make any money on seniors, and anyway, they don't even know if they like them.

This is perhaps why brands such as Fila in the UK have no hesitation in running campaigns in which the voiceover to a picture of an old man and woman asks 'Any last request?', as though before dying the only intelligent thing they could do would be to buy a pair of Fila sport shoes. Would they have dared to do the same by making fun of gays or minority ethnic groups?

One thing is certain, tackling the over 50s market requires great tact and extreme prudence, because the 50+ consumer is experienced and demanding.

The aim of this book is to enable everyone to understand and become better acquainted with this individual in order to be able to establish a profitable over 50s marketing strategy within the business.

CHAPTER 2

Unavoidable generational marketing

There can be no doubt that of all the criteria that explain a consumer's behaviour pride of place must go to his (or her) age and generation. The record shows that the American team at the research group headed by Dan Yankelovitch was the first to talk about generational marketing at the end of the 1960s. They had been commissioned by the anxious management of Playtex, who were concerned at the collapse of the sales of their corsets, to identify the generation-related behaviour of their customers. In fact, according to the traditional analysis of the 4 Ps of the marketing mix, everything appeared normal. The Product was of excellent quality, the Price was well positioned and consistent with its quality, the Promotion (or Publicity) quite sufficient with a media target of both younger and older women, and the Placing (distribution) of the product was efficiently spread over the nation through numerous attractive outlets. Everything was normal and yet sales of corsets continued to decline. Yankelovich's team concluded that this marketing problem had to be tackled from a different angle – the generation. The American baby-boomers' generation were reaching the age where they wanted to wear more elaborate underwear and they had no intention of wearing the same type of garment as their mothers.

The members of this generation had very definite views of what they thought was fashionable and sexy. They had decreed that the corsets were certainly not comfortable and free enough for their lifestyle. When their mothers tried to persuade them to wear this type of underwear they were treated as 'has-beens'. Worse still, the mothers themselves were beginning to be influenced by their offspring and to have doubts about their own dress habits, such was the influence of the baby-boom generation that it was already beginning to dictate the dress code for all.

The Yankelovich group's conclusion was to recommend to Playtex to respond rapidly to the needs and tastes of this growing generation that wanted more freedom of movement. The brand abandoned all its stiff whalebones and rubber stays in favour of lighter, softer, suppler bras, and sales took off once again. Generational marketing was born.

The first basic consumer segmentation in order to establish a generational marketing strategy of course involves an analysis of the age of the target market. Life is a succession of stages. Moreover, popular wisdom tells us: 'there is a time for everything', 'you are not old enough', 'I'm too old for this'. Ultimately, we pay homage to a chronological order of things, before class or lifestyle. Man must move with the times. He must manage his personal life to the best of his ability and at the same time ensure the survival of his family group. Age is unquestionably the basic criterion for the structure of society. The cycle of life is such an obvious thing that marketing sometimes forgot about it altogether.

The three dimensions of age: biological, psychological and social

To make the analysis easier, one can envisage three dimensions of age:

- biological
- psychological
- social.

Biological age

Man has a biological clock. His development and ageing are programmed. Many deep-seated concerns that will have a strong influence on consumption are linked to ageing and will replace one another over time. Man's needs continue to be strongly associated with the fact that he is made up of flesh and blood. This biological dimension is fundamentally controlled by time, passing through the stages of growing up, the need to reproduce and raise children, ensure their future and, finally, to manage one's old age in the best possible conditions.

Psychological age

Biological maturity, alone, is insufficient to attain psychological maturity. Man has little instinct, but his intellectual capacity allows him to form his personality through learning. Human apprenticeship is written in time. We cannot acquire a supply of knowledge immediately (it is absorbed slowly). Learning is concerned with knowledge, but also with action; man learns essentially through mimicry.

A person's behaviour is a function of what is learnt, through experience or practice. We can therefore say that there is a psychological age that depends on what that person has been able to learn and do, but equally that depends on their capacity to improve their behaviour through experience (it is said that some people will never understand anything). And then, of course, one's psychological age is something that one feels one has. It is a well-known fact that when one is a child one wants to be older and would easily add ten years to one's age, but when one is over 50, one likes to reduce the biological age by 10 to 15 years. The spirit feels much younger than the flesh.

Social age

Age is strongly affected by society. First, society controls time. The transfer to adulthood is ratified by society, (for example, women were for a long time considered to be minors in Europe and still are in many parts of the world). It is therefore not enough to be able to do such and such a thing, one also needs society's consent, and that begins with parental consent.

We should finally recall that a person's routine is linked closely to his age. For example, even if the obsessional target of TV programme planners is those buying for the able-bodied under 50s, the fact remains that because they are working, they are not, by far, the front-line TV viewers. As a reminder, we should note that more or less uniformly throughout the developed countries, those over 60 watch on average more than four hours of TV per day (that is, two hours more than the target audience of 25–35-year-olds), because they are free of all the constraints that organise and regulate our days.

Pre-eminence of age over all other segmentation criteria

Every product or service is in fact aimed at a target of selected consumers that will have specific characteristics, owing to the fact that it assumes some moment in the consumer's routine, some culture, some knowledge or even some sanction from society.

For example, it is quite clear the consumption of health products or services correlates very strongly with biological age (whether clients or patients). Conversely, the consumption of cultural benefits, such as the theatre or literature, will be more significantly influenced by the psychological or social age.

Age has a noticeable effect on the needs of consumers in many domains. Conversely, other markets are relatively linear throughout life, such as food products, for example, since we all need to eat. Nevertheless, even for a market that involves everyone, segmentation by age is often relevant because it facilitates more finely tuned, and therefore more effective, marketing and advertising. An example is the lower-fat cheese range from the Bongrain Group in France called 'Fine Bouche', which is apparently aimed at everyone. Some years after its launch on to the French market, the brand discovered that it was achieving a higher consumption rate among the over 50s, who found in this product the right balance between taste and lightness (health concerns are always stronger among the over 50s than in any other age group). The brand decided to take advantage of this natural phenomenon by creating a TV 'infomercial' designed to appeal directly to the over 50s and broadcast exclusively during the day over two TV channels with many 50+ viewers. With a very modest budget (about 300,000 euros per year), sales volumes increased by nearly 40% in the months following the campaign. Thanks to this strategic choice, the brand became leader of its market sector in two years.

In the USA, from the 1920s while the Model T Ford (archetype of the 'one-model-for-all' system) accounted for 55% of the automobile market, General Motors had adopted a radically different strategy chosen to divide its range of brands according to the age of its clientele. The essential idea was that for each stage of an individual's life there was a price range, together with a certain standard of comfort and equipment. This strategy was presented as 'A car for every purse and purpose'. Each brand had its target age of consumer, from the cheapest Chevrolet (for the young and less well off), through the Pontiac, Oldsmobile, Buick, up to the top of the range, with the Cadillac (for the old and rich).

When a person is young, a car must project a certain image and at the same time have room to transport friends. Later, it must serve to accommodate child seats and frequent trips to the supermarket. Afterwards, it must show that one has reached a certain social status while still remaining in the know and continue to retain the criteria of handling, safety, comfort and size. All of this corresponds to the broad majority behaviour of car buyers in 2002, including more unusual behaviour that is beginning to appear, for example, those over 50s who go for the smart 'young' small cars, such as the Twingo from Renault, the Yaris from Toyota, or even the Smart.

Every marketing manager is constantly looking for the most relevant and operational criteria for building a target market. It is quite clear that biological age is one, if not the key, criterion that drives consumer behaviour. Above all, it has the advantage of being simple, real and easy to bring into play in terms of media planning. Simplicity is a basic virtue in marketing!

When age is used as the central criterion for segmentation one realises that it is in fact statistically the most appropriate tool for drawing up the reasonably accurate model of the targeted consumer. It will therefore be relatively easy for the marketing manager to extrapolate the economic situation, financial resources, main needs as to equipment and services, preferred retail outlets, the best time to advertise, and so on.

A fairly recent instance of the primacy of age over all other criteria for explaining behaviour was shown in the French study by Credoc in September 1998 for the International Longevity Centre, France, called 'The baby-boom children face up to their future'. This study is exciting because it sets out to compare three age groups across a very large number of criteria and values. A group of younger over 50s (which we call the Liberated), aged from 60–64 is compared with two groups of baby boomers, the older aged 50–54 and the other 45–49. It is very instructive to see how the 1968 generation, with the reputation of being especially questioning and modernistic in its values, behaves and expresses itself when it approaches advanced middle age (that is, 50).

Values of the baby-boom generation

What are the values that you are most attached to and would wish to pass on? (Table 2.1.)

We will quote the comment on the surprising consistency in the replies from these three groups made by the study team:

> After rejecting authoritarianism, submission, intolerance, and praising freedom, autonomy and independence, the children of the baby-boom era finally settled for pursuing the same aims as their parents – namely, honesty, respect, the work ethic and the family. The baby-boom generation blamed their parents for being too rigid and excessively strict in the parent/child relationship

Table 2.1 The values to pass on			
Age of interviewee	45–49 years	50–54 years	60–64 years
Honesty	31.3	32.7	33.7
Work (ethic)	22.1	22.7	21.9
Family	21.1	21.3	23.9
Education	16.4	13.3	12.1
Politeness	8.2	5.3	5.0
Solidarity	11.9	9.7	6.3
Source: Credoc, France, 1001 persons, July 1998			

and complained of a lack of freedom in numerous areas of their daily life. Paradoxically, they have adopted the values that they judge to be those of their parents and wish to pass them on to their children without however, abandoning the primordial value for which some of them claimed to have struggled, namely, liberty.

This comparison points up the importance of age and the life cycle where behaviours and attitudes are concerned.

Bernard Préel, director of the BIPE (Bureau d'Information et Prévision Economique) is one of the greatest European specialists on generation behaviour and author of the remarkable book, *le choc des générations*, which appeared in 2000. He has refined this concept of the life cycle thus:

If age retains an explanatory value, it is not chiefly because it is the reflection of a biological factor (that of arteries and neurones), but because it is linked with stages of life, a life cycle that fluctuates (the start and end dates move appreciably) and revolves around two axes:

■ The axis of private (family) life, with its changes of state that punctuate the course of life: leaving home, celibate life, pairing, children, children leaving home, solitary life of the survivor

■ The axis of public (professional) life, with its classic periods: training, working, retirement.

The main ages of life are fixed and so the life cycle is marked out, by identifying the breakpoints that change the state and the critical moments that cause a period of instability.

So, Bernard Préel has created a life cycle of six ages which presents a synthetic view of the life of every person.

Figure 2.1 shows how the traditional breakdown of life into three periods (youth, activity and old age) is no longer suitable at the beginning of the twenty-first century. We are faced rather with three types of age that consist of a cycle of six periods, each theoretically lasting 15 years:

■ Two ages of dependence, childhood and old age, when one is strongly dependent on others

■ Two ages of great freedom, when individuals are no longer forced, as in the past, to carry out some professional activity even though they still have the physical faculties for it; youth on the one hand and retirement on the other. The greatly increased duration of these two periods with favourable standards of living represent a marketing opportunity for all businesses. Here we have a worldwide pool of consumers who are enjoying life, are in good health and are able to take full advantage of this new freedom, generally with ample financial means or the power to make decisions. These two target markets, the younger and the older, are especially attractive

■ Two ages of professional activity, symbolically separated by a turning point that is located at the mid-point of life and which coincides quite well with the peak of a career and the moment when the children take off on their own.

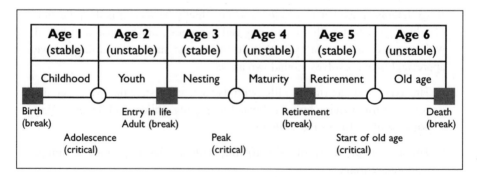

Figure 2.1 Bernard Préel's life cycle of six ages

Source: BIPE, December 1998

If we take the example of France, according to the latest evaluations carried out by Insee, the French institution of statistics, for the next 20 years, the growth of manpower of these different age groups is markedly in contrast. Significant decline in the first three categories: infancy –7.4%, youth –6.6% and nesting –8.9%, whereas after 45, the manpower of the other categories increases spectacularly: maturity +29.1%, retirement +36% and notably old age with a leap of +71.2%.

Grouping the age categories according to the suggested criteria gives a new configuration of French society on the 2020 horizon in three groups made up as follows:

- Dependency: Childhood (16.8%) + Old age (9.5%) = 26.3% of population

- Liberty: Youth (18.2%) + Retirement (17.3%) = 35.5% of population

- Production: Nesting (18.5%) + Maturity (19.7%) = 38.2% of population.

This situation will be very similar in the vast majority of developed countries, in North America and Asia, and of course in the old continent of Europe.

Enrich the age through generation

We need to refine the analysis because human beings are so complex and it is necessary to add a dynamic dimension to the basic concept of age that generational marketing can bring into play. It is quite clear that a man of 60 who retires today has little in common with the 60-year-old who retired 30 years ago, any more than an adolescent of 15 today and his alter ego of 20 years ago would have much in common. They are all at the same stage in life, and yet their behaviours are in many respects very different. The chief reason for this is clear: the two pensioners and the two adolescents belong to totally different generations.

> You would commit a serious error if you were to deduce that because your consumers reach a certain age they will behave in the same as those that reached that age at an earlier time. (J.W. and A. Clurman, Yankelovitch, USA)

So, any marketing manager who assumed that the baby boomers (those born between 1946 and 1964) would on reaching their 60th birthday abandon the Rolling Stones, Jimmy Hendrix, Eric Clapton or Genesis,

stop drinking Coca-Cola, no longer wear jeans or begin to under-consume
like the very old, would be drawing generally false commercial conclusions. He or she would be forgetting that the characteristic consumption
dynamic of the baby boomers and their music, dress and eating preferences will stay with them to their graves. For one of the spectacular
contributions of generational analysis has been to demonstrate that in old
age people remain broadly faithful to the lifestyle, values, objects and
music that they adopted, used or liked when young.

Another French study carried out by Insee 'Consumption, savings,
income: recent behaviour and trends', published at the end of 1999, was
able to show the importance of the differences in behaviour between
consumers belonging to different generations. Many pessimists are in
fact concerned about the negative consequences that an ageing population might have on European consumption in 15 years' time, so strong is
the idea that the older one gets, the less one consumes. The study by the
Insee researchers shows that nothing is less certain and that the oldest
current generations exhibit a less dynamic behaviour because they have
suffered hardship in their youth. 'The decrease in consumption after 70 is
therefore partially explained by the inclusion of households aged over 50
along with generations that have always had the habit of consuming
less.' Insee embarked on the task of comparing not the consumption of
current 70-year-olds with those who are currently 45, but, on the
contrary, comparing what they would have consumed in 1960 for
example. The result is revealing: 'Two households with the same income,
of the same size and with the same qualifications, but whose members
were born 60 years apart (1900–04 and 1960–64) thus have at the same
age a 12–20% variation in consumption, depending upon the level of
education.' This study gives grounds for strong optimism on the future
consumption of the new over 50s, since they will be the children of
generations that have lived through the consumer society. Insee
concludes that ageing certainly does not necessarily correlate with
a collapse in consumption. In 1979, spending of 70–74-year-olds
amounted to between 67% and 91% (according to qualification) of that
of 40–44-year-olds. In 2004, Insee predicts that this proportion will be
between 82% and 90%.

Key concept of the generation cohort

During the course of the second half of the twentieth century our society to
some degree invented the idea of 'youth' by broadening the duration of this

period of unconcern and 'irresponsibility'. In fact, up until then, except in the favoured sectors found in all countries (nobility, eminent people, the intellectuals and the middle classes), people moved directly from childhood to productive work. (We should remember that this remains the norm in the overwhelming majority of developing countries where children aged 6–7 begin work in factories or the street in order to make their essential contribution to the needs of the family.) The duration of the period of youth continues to increase, and takes on a growing importance in the psychological education of the young men and women of our Western societies. We are witnessing increasing delay in the decision-making of our young people. Formal unions are put off (the average marrying age will soon exceed 30), having the first child is delayed as long as possible, and embarking on a professional career is put back (on this point, we should concede that this may not be entirely from choice). In short, the young are able to settle comfortably in a world of great freedom, where choice is not a priority and they are all the more receptive to all kinds of influence, emotion and experience that find in them a particularly fertile breeding ground. Bernard Préel used the term 'impressionable time' to describe this stage in life.

This state of perpetual adolescence will sooner or later become *the* reference culture of our society, since it is so true that most of the time one looks back nostalgically to one's youth and considers oneself mentally younger than one is physically.

For many years sociologists and statisticians have put forward the idea of a cohort,[1] by showing that members of the same generation are linked closely by common experiences that marked their youth indelibly. Such events (war, depression, revolution, a major cultural change, a fundamental technological change) occurring during the formative years of youth will influence strongly consumers of the same age throughout their lives. Do we not continue, more than 30 years later, to speak of the 1968 generation when referring to 50-year-olds whose spirit of independence or non-respect for authority remain dominant traits of their character? How can one not be equally struck by the instinctive reaction of many older pensioners (the 'peaceful' and the 'elderly', that is, the 75–85 age group and those over 85) to stock up with basic essentials, such as sugar, pasta and canned food, as soon as there is any sign of national social conflict, as occurred during the French public transport strike of the SNCF and RATP in the winter of 1995? This was a reaction caused by the memory of the food shortages they had experienced in their youth and not owing to a real risk of shortage in our era of superabundant food supplies and highly organised distribution systems.

The influence of events that occurred during formative years is such that, even if circumstances evolve in a significant fashion, the individual remains largely conditioned by what he or she has lived through and learnt in the first 25–30 years of life. To quote Bernard Préel:

> Youth has not yet acquired its lobster shell to protect itself … it is the age when one is most easily upset, most vulnerable and feels the force of experiencing things for the first time. It is also the age when values are established, sometimes for life. This is how the great emotions of youth will permeate a generation.

J. Walker Smith and Ann Clurman of Yankelovitch partners have illustrated the main generation influence factors that determine our consumption behaviour (see Figure 2.2).

Of course, each generation will pass through the same stages of life: adolescence, obtaining driving licence, first job, having children, retire-

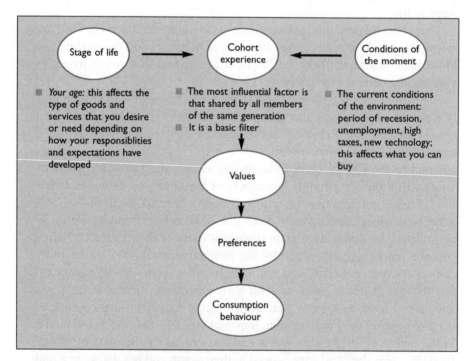

Figure 2.2 Influence factors that determine consumption behaviour

Source: Rocking the Ages, J. Walker Smith and A. Clurman

ment. Likewise, whatever generation we belong to, we face similar events: economic crisis, political crisis, wars. Nonetheless, the members of each generation will react in a somewhat different way to each of these events, depending on the values and reflexes that come from their experience at the heart of the generation cohort. The 'culture' of a generation is linked strongly to the radical changes in the environment that occurred during the formative years of the members of that generation. The members of a generation resemble one another not only because they are at the same stage of life, but also because this stage of life unfolds at the same time.

The importance of generation markers

Generation markers is the name given to the symbolic facts that have profoundly left their mark on the collective memory of the young belonging to that generation. So, for the older retirees, some of the most significant markers will have been the First World War, the 1929 Stock Market crash, the rise of Nazism, the Second World War, the Indian War of Independence, and so on. For the baby boomers, the markers would have been the consumer society, the Vietnam War, the arrival of colour TV, supermarkets and self-service, sexual freedom and, of course, in France and many other European countries, May 1968. For the young, known as the 'kangaroo' generation (because they like to stay safe and warm at home with their parents for as long as possible), the markers would be AIDS, divorce, MTV, Gameboy, the PC explosion and the Internet revolution.

When one wants to understand a person, it is important to know his or her history: one needs to get inside their skin and their head. It is the experiences that unite those who have lived them and which transcend social barriers. A person born in 1938, with childhood memories of the Second World War and the hard years that followed, will have more things in common with a person born in 1919 than with a person born in 1948. In the same way, a person born in the years when everything seemed easy, during the so-called '30 glorious years' (roughly 1945 to 1973), will find it much more difficult to adapt to the new economic order than a person born during the years of recession and economic crisis that followed them.

We can therefore quite fairly summarise the differences between the epochs by analysing the elements that symbolise them. We can also summarise a generation by using the markers of the epoch during which it was formed, that is, the first 15–20 years of the members that go to make it up.

This is the basis that some generation specialists have used to distinguish different generations by starting with a significant marker from their epoch, so true is it that these events have fashioned a quite specific culture that is common to the young people of the epoch. Generation markers represent as many 'breaks' that will equally have as their consequence the creation in turn of a break between the members of these generations and those of other generations that have not necessarily experienced them with the same intensity. The contemporaries of a generation cohort came together while putting up barriers with other generations. We thus witness a clear tendency to stretch the vertical links through which old values are transmitted for the benefit of a reinforcement of the horizontal links between persons who have experienced the same events. It is well known that members of the younger generation make it a point of honour not to accept the authority of their elders quietly and challenge the values that the latter would like to see them adopt. They will on the contrary devote considerable energy to imposing their own view of things on other generations. One of the chief difficulties that the marketing manager encounters when implementing a marketing target based on age criteria is the quite natural propensity to extrapolate the behaviours and reactions of this target from a personal point of view. Everyone imagines (more or less unconsciously) that the consumer will react to the marketing or advertising stimulus that the brand sends in much the same was as they themselves do. This is clearly the best way of missing the target! (This is also what goes to make the approach through generational marketing more complex: this partially explains why very few marketing and advertising managers are interested in it.)

The offbeat humour of an advertising spot devised by young creative people and accepted by young marketing managers (average age 30) has a good chance of making young consumers howl with laughter, while profoundly irritating the over 50s who expect factual information in order to become interested in a product.

Note

1. According to Claudine Attias-Donfut, acknowledged specialist on generations, the distinction between the classes of age, cohort and generation is based on the criterion of the interval of years considered: a few years for the age class, ten years for the cohort, 24 years for the generation.

CHAPTER 3

A silver-haired population

Ageing – an inescapable wave

It is rare to find surprises in the field of demographic statistics. Rapid ageing of the population of economically developed countries has been apparent for a long time. The rhythm of this ageing is speeding up. Two figures are striking illustrations of this phenomenon: between 1990 and 2020, the strength of the under 50s, in Europe, is set to increase by only 1%, whereas that of the over 50s will explode, with a growth of more than 75%. According to the predictions produced by the US Census Bureau, between 1997 and 2025 the world population will increase by 36%, during which time the number of people aged 60+ will grow by 112% and those aged 80+ by more than 152%.

The improvement in life expectancy is quite incredible. Consider also the fact that two-thirds of those who have reached the age of 65 since the beginning of mankind are living today!

In the world, if the number of over 60s amounted to 500 million in 1990, they rise to 600 million in 2000 (the current population of the African continent), and become 1.1 billion in 2020 (the current population of China). (Figure 3.1.) As a percentage, there are 30 countries in the world where those over 60 account for more than 15% of the population.

Contrary to what many people believe, ageing is not a unique phenomenon restricted to the developed countries. It concerns the world population across all continents. To give two examples, between now and the year 2025 in Brazil the population share of over 65s will grow by 365% (moving from 5.2% to 19% of the total) whereas in the UK the increase in share will 'only' be 34%. As for China, it is already the largest 50+ market in the world with 59 million people over 65 in 1990, and this sector is set to explode in numbers during the next decades. So, according to an article that

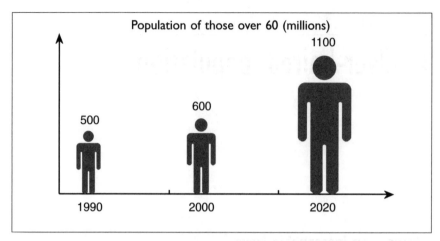

Figure 3.1 Ageing of the population is a worldwide phenomenon
Source: Senioragency

appeared in the main North China newspaper, the *Liaoning Daily*, in June 2001, by 2050 China will have more than 400 million individuals aged over 60, including 80 million over 80! Also, from having 6681 centenarians in 1981 the figure will have risen to more than 470,000 by 2050.

As a consequence, the age of the population of the different zones will average 45 years. The three leading zones will be Europe, North America and, level pegging, Asia and Oceania (Figure 3.4).

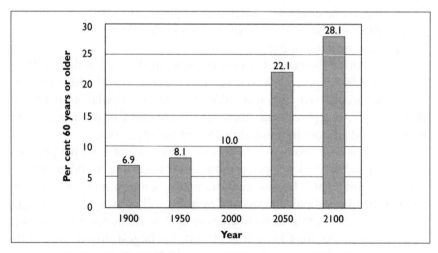

Figure 3.2 Three centuries of world population ageing
Source: Long-range World Population Projections. United Nations Secretariat

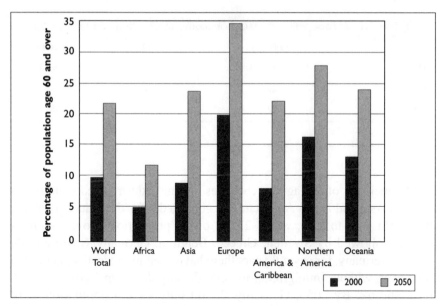

Figure 3.3 Percentage increase in age 60 and over by region, 2000–50

Source: Long-range World Population Projections. United Nations Secretariat

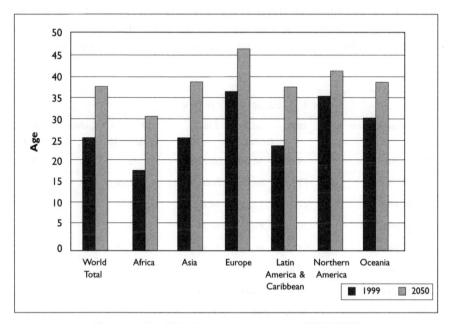

Figure 3.4 Median age by region, 1999–2050

Source: World Population Prospects. United Nations Secretariat

Table 3.1 Europe will increasingly become the bastion of the over 50s			
	1985 (%)	2000 (%)	2020 (%)
EU	30	33	41.5
USA	25.5	27.5	35
Japan	27	35.5	40
Source: Seniorscopie			

The majority of the ageing countries are the industrialised countries of Europe, Asia and North America. The gold medal for the oldest country in the world goes to Italy, where 22.2% of the population is over 60, to be closely followed by Sweden, Greece, Belgium, Germany, Spain and the UK. In Germany, for several years there have been more deaths than births; moreover, without immigration in 2000 the population in Germany would have shrunk. By 2050, Germany should only have a population of 65 million, compared with the figure of 82 million today.

There are three reasons for the growth in the number of people over 50: the post-war baby boom, the decrease in birth rate and the growth in life expectancy. At the end of the Second World War, no doubt to conspire against fate and forget all those years of war, hatred and death, our parents had an unbridled desire to procreate. At the same time, more or less all over the world (except in Germany and Japan), the fertility rate rose spec-

Table 3.2 European population by age group					
Age of population	2000	2020 (millions)	2050	Change in population between 2000–20	2000–50
0–14 years	64.19	58.63	52.23	−5.56	−11.96
15–29 years	73.96	66.18	58.52	−7.78	−15.44
30–44 years	87.17	72.60	64.25	−14.57	−22.92
45–59 years	70.52	86.10	68.28	+15.58	−2.24
60–74 years	54.51	67.46	65.96	+12.94	+11.45
75–89 years	24.63	33.75	34.91	+9.12	+10.28
90 and over	1.97	3.34	6.23	+1.37	+4.26
Total	376.96	388.06	366.96	+11.10	−10.00
Source: BIPE after Eurostat projection					

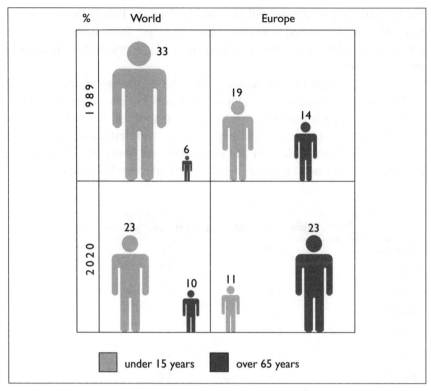

Figure 3.5 Old Europe

Source: Euroscopie

tacularly to about 3.8 children per woman. This baby boom lasted from 1946 to 1964, producing an 'avalanche' of babies, then adolescents and young adults. In the USA there were 76 million, nearly one American in three. The expression 'a pig moving through a python' has often been used to describe the phenomenon of the baby boom, which surprised all governments and authorities since they had made no preparations to receive, care for and educate this mass. That was in 1946. More than 50 years later, a similar phenomenon has occurred with the baby boomers reaching their 50s. Since 1 January, 1996 in the UK one person has reached the age of 50 every 50 seconds; in the USA the rate is one every seven seconds!

The ageing of a population increases more quickly as the number of births decreases. Now, the birth rate continues to decline worldwide, in both developed and underdeveloped countries. In order to see a growth in population, without immigration, the demographic status quo birth rate needs to be 2.1 children per woman; anything below this figure

means that the population will inexorably decline. This is the case in the
majority of developed countries (the average for Europe was 1.53
children in 2000), with the exception of the USA where the situation is
more satisfactory.

As far as lifespan is concerned, since the beginning of the twentieth
century the inhabitants of developed countries have seen on average 30
years added to their life expectancy, that is, as much as was achieved over
the preceding 5000 years! Throughout the twentieth century we have
gained two additional days of life expectancy for every week! According
to a report from Eurostat in August 2001, infant mortality continues to fall

Table 3.3 Total fertility rate per woman

Countries	2000	2025
USA	2.1	2.2
Canada	1.6	1.7
Germany	1.4	1.5
Spain	1.1	1.4
Italy	1.2	1.3
France	1.9	1.7
Sweden	1.5	1.6
Norway	1.8	1.8
Finland	1.7	1.7
Denmark	1.7	1.7
Japan	1.4	1.6
China	1.8	1.8
India	3.1	2.2
Indonesia	2.6	2
Singapore	1.2	1.5
South Korea	1.7	1.7
Taiwan	1.8	1.7
Thailand	1.9	1.7
Vietnam	2.5	2
Australia	1.8	1.7

Source: US Census Bureau, IDB Summary Demographic Data 2001

Table 3.4 Life expectancy at birth		
Countries	**2000**	**2025**
USA	77.1	80.6
Canada	79.4	82.2
Germany	77.4	81
Spain	78.8	81.8
Italy	79	81.8
France	78.8	81.8
Sweden	79.6	82.2
Norway	78.7	81.7
Finland	77.4	81
Denmark	76.5	80.5
Japan	80.7	82.9
China	71.4	77.4
India	62.5	70.9
Indonesia	68	74.9
Singapore	80.1	82.5
South Korea	74.4	79.2
Taiwan	76.4	80.4
Thailand	68.6	75.3
Vietnam	69.3	75.8
Australia	79.8	82.3

Source: US Census Bureau, IDB Summary Demographic Data 2001

Table 3.5 The senior boom is in fact a woman's boom	
Population type	**Percentage of women**
Under 50 years	49
50–59 years	51
60–74 years	55
75 years and over	64

Source: Senioragency International

Table 3.6 Our demography produces more widows than widowers (French example)		
French population 1999	Widowers	Widows
Under 20 years	207	1490
60 years and over	20,2000	1,072,000
75 years and over	323,000	1,798,000
Total population	525,000	2,873,000
Source: INSEE, 1999 Census		

everywhere. In the EU, the figures are 4.9 deaths in 1000 live births, compared with 12.4 in 1980 and 34.5 in 1960.

Certainly, this century has seen the greatest progress in life expectancy. The number of centenarians in France is a good illustration: there were 2000 in 1953, 3000 in 1988, 6000 in 1994, 10,000 in 2000 and in 2050 there should be 150,000. Out of every 100 girls born in 2002, it is estimated that 30 will reach the age of 100. In 2001, the life expectancy for Japanese women had reached an average age of 84.62 (77.64 for men).

Male mortality introduces a dissymmetry into the destinies. At 60 years and over, there are 142 women for 100 men, at 75 and over 191 women for 100 men and at 85 and over 281 women for 100 men. Death destroys couples, leaving many more widows than widowers (Table 3.6). This is a vital fact for marketing and communication executives. The products and services that are to be addressed to the over 50s must take it into account. Once they are widowed, women have to make decisions that, in most cases, were previously made by their husbands. This is especially true in the areas of finance, insurance and taxation, often dealt with by men. Knowing how to advise, offer a personalised service and be patient and attentive, are the key to successful communication with women over 50.

Segmentation of the over 50s market

To know someone properly, you need to have walked in his shoes for moons and moons. (Old Cherokee saying)

The terminology 'over 50s' is a convenient one to distinguish this new market from younger consumers. At the same time, it is reductionist because it suggests that it includes in the same category people as different as a man of 50 in active occupation and a retired woman of 80. To be more effective, generational marketing relies on a finely tuned knowledge of consumers.

The basic belief of 'mass-marketing' is to think that one can win over a maximum of consumers with an identical product and the same message aimed at all markets, what the Americans call 'carpet bombing' (a term from the Second World War). The vast majority of companies proceed in this way: there is the 30-second TV spot sent out at 19.55, just before the big news broadcast for the evening, in the hope that 'God will recognise his own' and all those targeted will stampede for the product the next day. Generational marketing adopts the opposite to this warlike approach that lacks all finesse and precision. In the era of laser-guided 'surgical strikes' (to use the Gulf War terminology), generational marketing demonstrates that it is infinitely more effective and economical than mass marketing. For at the beginning of the twenty-first century, how can one still believe that one can address all generations of consumers in the same way? What do an adolescent of 15, a mother of 35 and a young retired person of 60 have in common? Their bodies are not the same, their needs are not the same, their background and level of education are different, they do not have the same values and aspirations, nor do they have the same financial resources, they do not like the same type of music and do not identify with the same heroes or celebrities. In short, they rarely follow the media in the same way. Brands are beginning to discover the virtues of this more refined type of marketing, which nonetheless demands a high level of knowledge of the behaviour and aspirations of the core market to which they want to appeal.

This is why it is essential to segment the over 50s markets into categories that correspond to phases of life unanimously recognised by American and European experts on the subject.

Much debate, and sometimes many controversies, surround the segmentation of the huge population of the over 50s. For my own part, since 1989 I have identified six broad criteria that facilitate the organisation of this target market: age, income level, whether working or not, state of health, time available and generation. I exclude from my analysis 'lifestyle' or 'social style', because to apply them in practice has always seemed to me to be too much of a complicated and even illusory intellectual exercise. I am reminded that the first objective of a segmentation is to be the most practical and concrete to permit the implementation of marketing actions. The six criteria therefore enable the 50+ group to be well identified and outlined. But six is already too high a number to achieve a simple result that is easy to implement. Could there be a determining criterion that would allow the other to be 'organised'? Yes is the answer, and it is the simplest and the most readily available: the criterion of age. We have in fact established from hundreds of different markets that if you know the age of the people you are addressing, you have a high level of reliability in the behaviours, needs and expectations, personal situations and generational state of mind of the segments thus formed. The watchword is to make it simple. Age is the most important of all the initial segmentation criteria for the over 50s.

Four marketing segments for the over 50s

We have defined these in Table 3.7.

Seeking out the Masters (50–59 years)

> Recently, I passed my fiftieth year. This is youth for a tree, the middle of life for an elephant; but it's old age for a former 400-meter runner whose son now tells him: 'Dad, I can no longer run with you unless I bring something to read!' (Bill Cosby, *When I was My Age*)

One's 50s are something like the Indian summer of life. Everything conspires to make this decade an exciting time of life. One has money (whatever job one has, one is at the peak of one's earning power), more free time, good health still, and the desires that one has not been able to satisfy so far are finally within reach. The only bad moment for the 50-year-olds

Table 3.7 Senioragency's four segments			
The Masters* **50–59 years**	**The Liberated*** **60–74 years**	**The Peaceful*** **75–84 years**	**The Elderly*** **85 years +**
In Europe 34 million in 1988	In Europe 41 million in 1988	In Europe, 22 million in 1988	
Will be 45 million in 2005	Will be 45 million in 2005	Will be 27.5 million in 2005	
The European market of over 50s comes to more than 120 million.			
*Terminology from Senioragency			

concerns women who have to endure the menopause (between 48 and 55 generally). This physical and psychological ordeal shows them irrefutably that they have just crossed another threshold in life. The journalist Nicci Gerrard described what she felt in the *Japan Times* in September 2000:

> The menopause, all those hormones charging around the body, often makes women feel jittery, panicky, hot, weepy, dreary and scared. But it also makes us depressed because the change reminds us how we are crossing over a line, from fecundity to barrenness. No wonder so many women have late pregnancies: it's a way of holding back the stage of life, trying to stay put. For older women are no longer objects of desire.

Of course, the new Master women belonging to the baby-boom generation will have much greater access to hormonal replacement therapy and other palliatives such as soya phytoestrogens, than their older sisters. As a result, they will suffer much less discomfort; post-menopausal women will feel much happier.

The Masters are clearly a preferred marketing target. At the very start of this decade, three major factors influence the consumption behaviour of the Masters:

■ The mortgage on the main residence is paid off (on average at 49). Usually lasting 15 to 20 years, this loan has been a heavy burden on the available income in the household (on average amounting to 25% to 33%), especially in European countries, where property is such a cornerstone of family life. People are prepared to suffer in order to build up a legacy

■ Now that they are grown up, the children leave the family home (on average when the mother is 52 and the father 54). This offspring has been expensive. Apart from bearing the costs of bringing them up for 25 years, it has been necessary to ensure that the children gained the education to enable them to succeed.

At the same time, it should be noted that there are several phenomena that prevent a clear separation between young adults and their parents. The baby-boomer generation has popularised divorce more than any previous generation. The 'mid-life crisis' has provoked a phenomenon, called by the Americans 'new nesting', more or less everywhere in the world. One begins a new life in one's 40s or 50s, has a new family (it is not unusual to find fathers who are grandfathers and new fathers). Another phenomenon is the difficulty that many young adults have in entering the world of work owing to regular crises on the job front.

Owing to the psychological stress that it brings, unemployment obliges parents to support their children financially who in turn enjoy the security of the family home and are inclined to put off their entry into the attractive world of work. For example, in France in 1985, 30% of boys and 42% of girls were receiving further and higher education; in 1996, the figures had risen to 52% and 72%.

This type of long-term student, who pursue their studies indefinitely, has emerged during the past decade or so. Even when the first job has been found, it is not unusual to find them still living with their parents. It is so much more convenient to be housed, fed, have one's laundry done, be pampered by one's mother, and to receive a salary on top that allows one to buy what one wants!

This new sociological phenomenon has been dubbed the 'kangaroo generation', because young adults continue to remain under the protection of their parents (in the protective 'pouch'). Here, we will quote from 'The state of world population', 1998, presented by the United Nations Population Fund:

> Children who leave the parental home to study or live with friends frequently return, even those who leave on marriage may be back, not to give succour to their ageing parents, but to seek support after divorce ... parents keep paying, being involved.

Although not statistically negligible, this phenomenon does not apply in the majority of situations. Fortunately for the Masters, they do eventually achieve some relief.

■ Again, with the increased expectation of life, the age of the heirs becomes increasingly greater. (In the West the average age for inheritance has grown from between 47 and 48 years 15 years ago to between 51 and 53 years today.) People are therefore often over 50 themselves when they inherit

This age range will therefore enjoy new disposable income (said to be an increase of more than 30%) and be interested in high quality goods and services that were hitherto beyond their reach

■ They will give priority to purchases that make life comfortable (house, equipment, car, second home, leisure electronics, and so on)

- They enjoy a quality standard of living (restaurants, boutiques, dietetics, organic foods). In clothing, they buy designer labels and made to measure

- As for travel, all those longed-for trips are now within reach. But these Masters are by no means 'grasshoppers', about to squander away all the wealth they have amassed as 'ants'. They know the value of money and they will continue to save some of it for their old age and for their children. They are very valuable clients for financial organisations and insurance companies

- Finally, we cannot fail to mention the powerful urge felt by the members of this age group to fight against the ravages of time. Cosmetics, physical exercise, low-fat diets, neutraceutics and, increasingly, cosmetic surgery which becomes more widespread as the baby boomers grow in age. Spreading from the USA, where there were 500,000 operations in 2000, compared with 180,000 in 1992, this fashion is growing ever stronger. The average age for a face-lifting operation has decreased from 50 in 1990 to 42 today. Liposuction is developing at speed (doubling in five years with more than 200,000 treatments). As *Business Week* stated in March 1998:

> The oldest baby boomers are now in their fifties and they are fighting the onslaught of age with the same doggedness as they showed when they demonstrated as young people.

We will discuss the considerable consumer power of the Masters in the next chapter.

Table 3.8 Some famous Masters

Name	Age (years)
Phil Collins	50
Richard Gere	52
Bill Clinton	56
George W. Bush	55
Mick Jagger	56
Paul McCartney	57
Catherine Deneuve	58
Julio Iglesias	58

Seeking out the Liberated (60–74 years)

> Youth! Youth! There is absolutely nothing in the world but youth! (Oscar Wilde)

Freed from work, freed from the need to educate their children, the over 60s discover their new freedom and begin a quite different life from what they have lived so far. This revolutionary change confuses some and excites the vast majority. The hope of living longer grows, with a long vista opening up.

Various pieces of international research, starting from the beginning of the twentieth century, illustrate the striking increase in life expectancy, once a person has retired. These show a constant progression that is even more impressive than the overall increase in life expectancy. (Table 3.9)

It is reasonable to think that our over 50s will soon be spending more than a quarter of their lives in retirement. Moreover, it will soon not be possible to believe that our economic practice can afford to drive so many people from the work place as soon as they are 50. The development of policies of early retirement and other forms of social treatment of unemployment has been so significant that in France, Germany, Belgium and Holland, there is less than one worker in three who moves straight from employment to the status of pensioner. France emerges as the country where the percentage of those aged 55–64 still in employment is the lowest of all the large economies. The figure is only 37%, compared with 53.3% in the UK, 59% in the USA and 66% in Japan (as in 1999). This situation is known to be explosive, as much for the social systems (the financing of pensions) as for a large number of over 50s who find that they are barred from work when they could be of service to the community. As former US congressman Claude Pepper stated:

> Age-based retirement arbitrarily severs productive persons from their livelihood, squanders their talents, scars their health, strains an already overburdened social security system, and drives many elderly people into poverty and despair. Ageism is as odious as racism and sexism. (*New York Times*, July 1997)

Table 3.9 Growth in life expectancy after retirement								
	1900	1940	1950	1960	1970	1980	1990	2000
Life expectancy after retirement years	1.2	9.1	11.6	13.6	14.5	16.4	18.5	20.5

Source: Senioragency International, based on BIT, USA Census Bureau

CE NE SONT
PAS DES
POLÉMIQUES
QUI VONT
PAYER MA
RETRAITE.

VISUAL: Polemics aren't going to pay my pension

The crunch time for the financing of pensions can be predicted to occur in 2005 when the first children of the baby boom finally leave the labour market at a rate two to three times faster than at present.

The campaign by the Cité Européenne in France was the first to focus on this serious problem some years ago (see visual).

The problem of pensions will be on the agenda of many foreign governments for a long time. It is based on a set of social benefits obtained after many battles with authorities. It will therefore not be easy to acknowledge that these benefits no longer apply in an era characterised by an ageing population.

When Otto von Bismarck, as German Chancellor, established in 1881 the first pension system, he chose the age of 65 as the official age for retirement. We should remember that at the time the average life expectancy in Europe was about 45 years. There were about 40 workers for every retired pensioner. Clearly, there was then no risk in financing pensions and it seemed a good way of preventing a significant part of the population from becoming paupers and perhaps resulting in social unrest. Today, the situation is quite different, after 60 (the official retirement age in some countries, such as France and Japan) or 65 (retirement age in Canada, USA, Australia, Spain, Scandinavia, Germany, Mexico, and so on), a pensioner has a long period of life that will have to be financed, either wholly, or in part, by the nation. This is, as we know, henceforth impossible, given the rapid and spectacular decline in the ratio of workers to pensioners (Table 3.10). In the future, politicians will have to find the courage to extend the official retirement age everywhere.

At the psychological level, a large proportion of Liberated pensioners are condemned to an enforced idleness that is known to be the cause of many divorces and deaths during the first two years of retirement. Finding himself suddenly rendered useless and rejected, a man turns round and sows dissension in his home, a domain that up until then was in the hands of his spouse.

For several years, the very powerful American Association of Retired Persons (discussed in detail in Chapter 6) has been running a huge campaign calling upon companies to employ over 50s under the banner 'Brain child'. Relayed by the American Labor Office, this campaign is the first of its kind. It presents a problem that concerns all ageing industrialised countries (see visual).

At the age of 60, one encounters a new life without imposed constraints or timetables. Time is conquered. Throughout the world, there are magazines, such as *Modern Maturity* (USA), *Yours, Choice, Saga Magazine* (UK) (see visual), *Notre Temps,* (see visual) *Pleine Vie* (France), *Club 3* (Italy), *Plus* (the Netherlands) and *Vi over 60* (Norway), that have cleverly contrived to make themselves essential reading for people in this exciting period of their lives.

All the stress built up during the 'eat–work–sleep' years gradually gives way to a new rhythm. This availability that we all lack is an important factor in the selling of goods and services to the Liberated. They can take their time to analyse the situation, study it from every angle, compare offers, read the literature, and discuss the matter with salespeople whose patience and comprehensions they can test to the limit. For this reason, those promotions that stress urgency, such as 'Offer valid 24 hours only', will have little attraction for them. This must be borne in mind.

The Liberated person is therefore a thoroughly experienced consumer who favours quality. We should never forget that such a person has often been the victim of shaky marketing schemes with its army of dubious products and shoddy items, quickly produced and badly produced, as well

Table 3.10 Estimate for developed countries		
1960	1990	2020
I pensioner for 4.6 workers	I pensioner for 2.2 workers	I pensioner for 1.5 workers
Source: Senioragency International		

VISUAL: AARP is actively lobbying on this crucial issue

as the temporary that lasts. They have greater confidence in the true known and established brands than all the generations. They are the 'brand victims' rather than the young. As they do not have debts and enjoy a good income (second out of all age groups), they are godsend for the tour operators and hotel chains. They are also in the sights of the high quality car manufacturers, as well as quality food producers, especially low-fat products, because health preoccupations figure increasingly in their thinking. During the menopause, women alter their diet appreciably, so as not to gain weight; coincidentally, the changed diet also benefits their spouse who is likely to be a little overweight. The catch phrase of the Liberated from now on is 'eat healthily to live long'. Being at the peak of their financial resources, they constitute a very attractive population for all the financial organisations and insurance companies, since a substantial part of the inheritance is in their hands. It is known that they have made a strong contribution to the success of state borrowings and privatisation issues. For one does not become a pensioner in order to throw money out of the window.

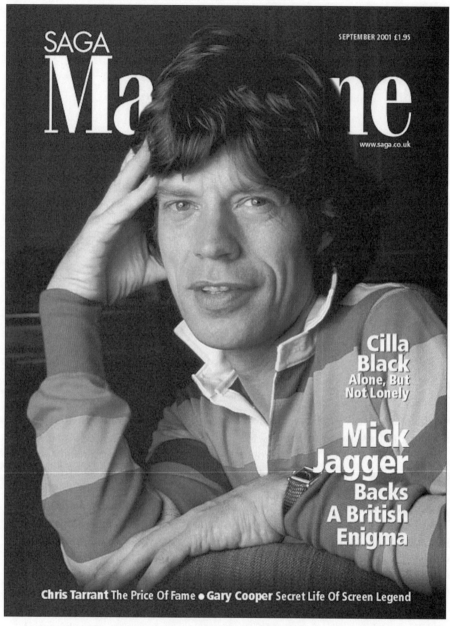

VISUAL: *Saga Magazine*, the magazine of the Saga Group, is the leading journal for the over 50s in the UK with a circulation of 1.1 million copies

At 60, one becomes more tolerant, more serene and more respectful of others. These new benevolent people will play an important role between the different generations. As they become moneyed grandparents (on average around 51–52), they acquire a new status, which is marvellous for themselves, their grandchildren and their children who can also rest a little and take advantage of some weekend breaks without any worries. So far as consumption is concerned, this new role will have consequences in a number of areas where the Liberated will invest notable sums: toys, games for the grandchildren, restaurants where they take them after seeing a show or a film. This does not escape the eyes of the large US corporations, such as Fisher Price, which sponsors a magazine called *Grandparents Today*, and profits from this manna. Equally, the New York store F.A.O. Schwarz, on Fifth Avenue, said to be the largest toyshop in the world, created its Grandma Shop, an area set aside for the over 50s to help them choose gifts that would really give pleasure to their grandchildren. We can also quote the tens millions of dollars invested by McDonald's in its worldwide campaigns that feature grandparents with their grandchildren in an attempt to overcome their reluctance to take them to fast-food restaurants. Disney, too, is also in the picture, and wherever its parks are established (USA, Japan Europe), runs campaigns that feature grandparents with their grandchildren.

The CNAV-INSEE study, carried out in France, showed that this generosity towards younger people could also take the more classic form of gifts of cash. Among the 68–92 age group, the sample studied by CNAV, close on 49% helped their children and grandchildren (excluding gifts). In 1997, INSEE calculated the amount of financial assistance given to family members as 6% of the household income at around 60 and 12% at around 80.

This is equivalent to 21 billion euros (including 5.3 billion in kind) transferred every year from the over 50s to their children and grandchildren. To put this aid in context, let us recall that in France the total amount of allowances distributed by the social security office (family allowances, accommodation allowances, RMI, and so on) amounted to 32 billion euros in 1994.

The over 50s are certainly the best social 'shock absorber' of our society in crisis. It can be estimated that, each year, they distribute, in one form or another, the equivalent of about one month's pension to the younger generations.

The Liberated spend a great deal on telecommunications, photography, cameras, and videos, and have increasingly launched into an exploration of the infinite potential of multimedia and the Internet. Since the beginning of

VISUAL: *Notre Temps,* the founder of senior magazines in Europe,
launched in May 1968 (sic!) it had a circulation of
1,050,000 copies per month as at January 2002

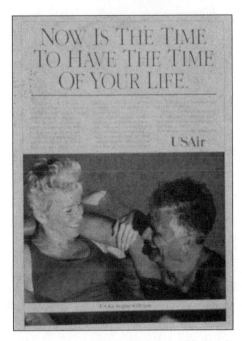

NOW IS THE TIME
TO HAVE THE TIME
OF YOUR LIFE.

USAir

VISUAL: USAir, like several American airlines, knows how to attract 50+ customers by a very delicate tone of communication

1998, IBM (see visual) has shown a particular interest in this market in the USA, where it has begun to advertise in *Modern Maturity* (the leading magazine aimed at this market). For some years, we have witnessed a tidal wave of over 50s surfing on the Web, not only as an instant rejuvenation course, but also as a way of demonstrating to oneself and to one's circle that one is 'on the ball' since one can handle the most symbolic tool of modernity.

Throughout the world, the fascination of the over 50s for the Web is striking. A study made by Dentsu in Japan in 2000 showed that 55% of the 60–74 age group 'want to use a personal computer and the Internet but don't know how'. In Sweden, according to Jupiter MMXI in the spring of 2001, in the 50–79 age group a total of 33% use the Internet. The age group represents 22% of the Swedish Internet surfers. A Swedish woman of 50 declared:

> It's fun to learn something new at our age. We are not just old fuddy-duddies. I think it builds up your self-confidence. (Bengal Consulting Senior report 2001)

Several large portals have been created to provide a generational response to the needs and expectations of over 50s surfers. In the USA,

VISUAL: IBM appeals to the desire for eternal youth among the over 50s –
'It's easy to become the most popular child in the neighbourhood'

www.thirdage.com; in the UK, www.vavo.com; in France and Belgium,
www.seniorplanet.fr. These sites have met with great success because they
have understood the specific needs of the 'silver' surfers. As Bill Gates
said about them, 'They don't surf on it, they deep mine on it!'

Table 3.11 A few celebrated Liberated individuals	
Name	Age (years)
Claudia Cardinale	62
Tina Turner	63
Sophia Loren	65
Luciano Pavarotti	66
Donald Sutherland	66
Elizabeth Taylor	67
Sean Connery	69
Clint Eastwood	69
James Brown	71
Paul Newman	73
Lauren Bacall	75

The Liberated have adopted all the modern tools of communication that enable them to keep in touch with their families. But, in order to satisfy these consumers, providers need to take account of the natural decline in physical capacities; sight and hearing deteriorate, physical actions become less precise; there is also psychological resistance, since, for many, modern technology remains incomprehensible. Few companies have appreciated this. We shall return to this topic in detail.

Seeking out the Peaceful (75–84 years)

Age improves four things: old wood, to provide a good fire, old wine, to be drunk, old friends, to give them confidence and old authors, for them to be read. (Francis Bacon)

Apart from a number of exceptions, some particularly brilliant (John Glenn went into space a second time at the age of 77), from the age of 75 one can say that one embarks on old age. The parameter of health becomes predominant, and it is this that affects the entire life of the Peaceful. However, one must beware of the perception that categorises 70-year-olds as people requiring care and assistance. Many of them are still fit and well. They have less energy and are sensitive to the slightest variations in diet or temperature, but they remain capable of living a more or less normal life.

The older one gets, the more the body machine can become disturbed. This can be caused by the death of a spouse. This comes as the ultimate test, since solitude can strike at one's morale, the essential spring of life. It is then that the social life of such individuals slows down. (The 70–80 decade is often considered to be the 'decade of death' for men.) They lose the taste for life. What use is their money or their free time? They feel that they have seen and done everything.

Statistically, this age group is largely inactive, and their average incomes are similar to those of young people embarking on a career. As a consequence, and for all the reasons already mentioned, one is faced with a class of consumer that is weakened, both psychologically and financially. They hardly spend money on anything more than food and health items, two areas that they believe strategically important. There is good potential in these areas for functional food products (lower fat foods, vitamins, fibre foods), for nutritional complements and palliative medicines, to give some examples.

Everything that could help to improve life at home interests them greatly. We see developing an important market in goods and services that

Table 3.12 Some well-known Peacefuls and Elderly	
Name	Age (years)
Tony Curtis	76
George Bush	77
John Glenn	79
Pope Jean-Paul II	81
Kirk Douglas	83
Ronald Reagan	90
Queen Elizabeth, the Queen Mother	101

enable the Peaceful to live in comfort and safety in their homes. Examples are stair lifts and walk-in baths and emergency communication systems in case of illness or a fall. Services that provide help in the home are destined to expand greatly in the future.

We should also remain alert to the constant increase in life expectancy that continues to push back the restrictions of ageing. Two or three decades ago, one was considered 'old' at 60; today, in the vast majority of cases, a 60-year-old is in 'full flower'. This suggests that, in 10 to 15 years, we shall have to advance this 75 age 'buffer' perhaps to 85.

Seeking out the Elderly (over 85)

Crabbed age and youth cannot live together:
Youth is full of pleasance, age is full of care;
Youth like summer morn, age like winter weather

Age, I do abhor thee; youth I do adore thee.

(William Shakespeare, 'The Passionate Pilgrim')

For many years, all the studies devoted to the health of old people have spoken of what is called the 'compression of morbidity', that is, the shorter the periods of illness, the longer one lives. This situation of general improvement is of benefit to all, but regrettably, the fact remains that, for a large number of people, the last years of life are characterised by a state of dependency. According to a study carried out by the Swiss group, Novartis

Pharma, in November 2000, across several European countries, 32.5% of people over 83 need permanent care in their daily lives. (In 1995, 19.7% of French people reported that they had an old close relation who was not independent.)

Dependency and solitude are the two keywords for this stage of life. Illnesses such as incontinency, Parkinson's or Alzheimer's disease are obviously the cause of considerable individual and family distress. These are likely to spread strongly in the coming years in all parts of the world affected by an ageing population. Apart from supporting a certain degree of dependence, the only solution that remains for many families is to place the aged relative in a specialist institution.

Yet we should not imagine that institutional life is the norm for the elderly. Thanks to the home care services and family solidarity, some two-thirds of those over 90 live at home, which is to the advantage of the individual and to society in general (for example, the development of new service initiatives).

SODEXHO, the giant international collective restaurant company, carried out in 2000 a huge study of 11 countries (including the USA, Brazil, Canada and many European countries) in order to be able to forecast better the foreseeable changes in lifestyle of the over 50s from now until 2025. One of the clear conclusions of the Sodexho Observer is that the pre-eminence of the home as the first place to live should not alter, but given the demographic age tidal wave the need for accommodation provided with the necessary services for people should explode (Table 3.13).

Health becomes the central preoccupation of this target market. Private companies can provide real solutions that improve the day-to-day

Table 3.13 Where will elderly people live?			
Living place	1999 %	2025 %	Change %
Home	83	86	+3
Family	11	6	−45.4
Medical establishments	4	4	None
Homes with services	2%	4	+100
Total	100	100	

Source: Sodexho observer 2000

life of the elderly. The lack of preparation on the part of our society for the massive build-up in the number of old people gives considerable scope for private initiative to alleviate the deficiencies of the public sector. This is especially true of retirement homes, of which there are notoriously too few; it is even more true in the case of care and assistance in the home.

Another notable characteristic of this age group is that it concentrates the number of financially disadvantaged pensioners. In fact, this population is largely made up of women many of them widows who only receive a reduced share of their dead husband's pension, since few women of this generation have worked to receive their own pension. A recent American study, carried out by the Life Insurance Marketing and Research Association, has demonstrated that widows face a 38% decline in household income after the death of their husband.

We have here a picture of this segment that, little by little, will be replaced by other pensioners whose status will be considerably improved in the years to come.

And this is only the beginning!

Let us give some thought to the striking figure of a further three months of life expectancy for children born each year in the future.

Thanks to plentiful food, of better quality, more balanced and healthy, the absence of major world conflicts for nearly 50 years, medicine that daily pushes illness further back, researchers who continue to discover new molecules (melatonin, DHEA), all of this brings to the populations of the richer countries the promise of a lifetime without fixed boundaries. Until today, biologist put man's maximum lifespan at 120 years. France has itself occupied a high place in the world ranks of centenarians with Jeanne Calment, who when she died in August 1997 had achieved the grand age of 122 years and six months. The British were able to celebrate with great enthusiasm the 101st birthday of their Queen Mother on 4 August, 2001.

We know that the basic cause of ageing is to do with the cell. In a newborn infant, the cells of the skin divide 50 to 60 times; in an adult, this rate falls to about 30; in an old person the division is no more than three or four. When there is no division, death occurs. This is why all gerontologists, biologists and geneticists (notably in the university campuses of California and New Mexico) are working on cells to find a solution that will enable the process of cell division to be prolonged as much as

Table 3.14 The different stages of life

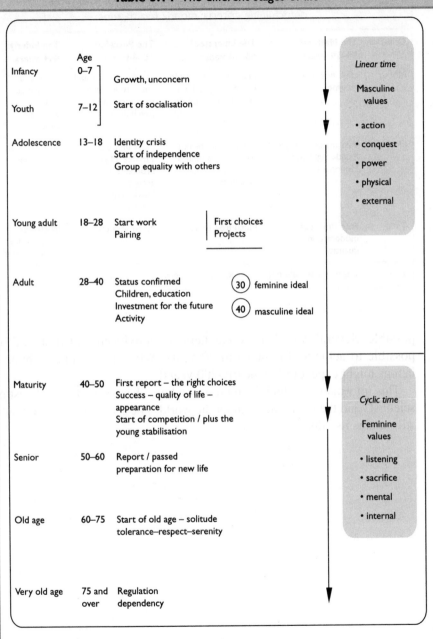

	Age			
Infancy	0–7	Growth, unconcern		**Linear time**
Youth	7–12	Start of socialisation		Masculine values
Adolescence	13–18	Identity crisis Start of independence Group equality with others		• action • conquest • power • physical • external
Young adult	18–28	Start work Pairing	First choices Projects	
Adult	28–40	Status confirmed Children, education Investment for the future Activity	(30) feminine ideal (40) masculine ideal	
Maturity	40–50	First report – the right choices Success – quality of life – appearance Start of competition / plus the young stabilisation		**Cyclic time** Feminine values
Senior	50–60	Report / passed preparation for new life		• listening • sacrifice • mental • internal
Old age	60–75	Start of old age – solitude tolerance–respect–serenity		
Very old age	75 and over	Regulation dependency		

Source: Qualitative study Les Séniors, WSA

50+ Marketing

Table 3.15 Life cycle of the over 50s based on the three determining criteria: money, health, time

Criterion	The Masters* 50–59 years	The Liberated* 60–74 years	The Peaceful* 75–84 years	The Elderly* 85+ years
Money	High disposable income	Maximum disposable income: the golden age of consumption	Weaker means and appetite for buying: (economic and psychological)	Many in a precarious state, especially widows
Health	Vast majority in good health. Sight declines. Menopause	Still in good health but sight continues to decline. Deafness	Most important variable. Physical problems are accentuated. Movements less precise	High level of dependency
Time	Free time, but moderate in quantity	Much free time	Much free time	Much free time, but no longer go out

Source: Senioragency International; * terminology from Senioragency International

possible. Several American researchers are convinced that it should be possible to achieve this in 10 to 20 years. When that happens, human beings might expect to live nearly 200 years!

This information, which is in no way a hoax, has excited the interest of scientists and the media throughout the world. The search for eternal youth still retains its allure.

CHAPTER 4

Consumption — the 50+ boom

50+ are not a share of the market;
they are a market share
JEAN MARC SEGATI, SENIORAGENCY INTERNATIONAL

Their financial resources

The income trustees

Through their disposable income and their inheritance, the over 50s hold a dominating position in the financial pyramid of households. 'Meagre, like the retirement of an old person' used to be a popular expression 30 years ago. Today it is incorrect; although they were once thought to be poor, now they are not. From corroborative studies carried out all over the world, the standard of living of those of 50 and over today exceeds that of younger people by an average of 30%. As a result of combing the official sources of many developed countries, it can be estimated that, in the mid-1990s in the large economies (USA, Japan, European Union), the over 50s, on average, collected some 43% of the net domestic income before tax, and they hold 50% of the net domestic inheritance. This domination will increase in 2005 to 50% of the net domestic income and 60% of the inheritance. The key concept of disposable income per unit of consumption (that is, relating to people living under the same roof) is very important, since it expresses the income available in a household where rates and taxes, and so on have been paid (see Table 4.1).

Table 4.1 Household disposable income by age group, on average, in developed countries (average = 100)

Age (years)	Disposable income per consumption unit
Under 26	81.8
26–30	92.5
31–40	97.0
41–50	99.4
51–60	104.9
61–65	107.8
66–70	112.5
Over 70	103.8

Source: Senioragency International (income calculated according to the Oxford unit consumption method)

Development of their purchasing power

The 50+ are undoubtedly the big winners in the financial and inheritance stakes over the past 20 to 30 years. After working hard for much of their

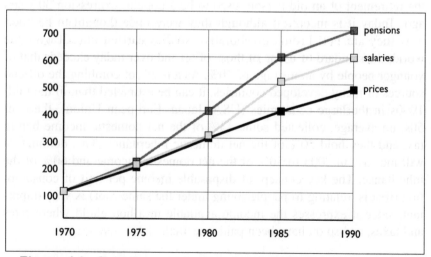

Figure 4.1 Growth in purchasing power of the over 60s in France
Source: CREDOC, France

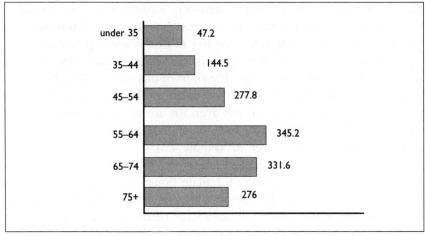

Figure 4.2 Mean net worth in the USA (in $1000)
Source: US Federal Reserve, 1995

life, helping to reconstruct the world after the terrible damage of the Second World War, they have been able to benefit from a significant improvement in their standard of living just as they reach pensionable age. We shall give some illustrations of this.

For example, in France, the purchasing power of the over 60s has increased seven times over 20 years, more than salaries (sixfold) and prices (fivefold) (see Figure 4.1).

In the USA, the same type of trend can be detected (Figure 4.2). The peak in income relates to the segments, Masters and Liberated, who stand out most prominently in the income scale.

Debts of the over 50s

It is well known that what allows the over 50s to enjoy comfortable incomes, is not so much that these incomes are higher than those of the younger generation (which is the case at the point of retirement), but the fact that throughout their life they have been able to build up an estate. In particular, this is achieved by buying their own home, car(s), even a second home (in their own country, or increasingly abroad). As a result, when one no longer has any debts to be repaid (a mortgage can easily involve a monthly outlay of 30% of income), one has a strong disposable income that can be spent on consumption, leisure or investment for an even better future or as a safeguard against any unexpected turn of events (such as a decrease in pension or the risk of illness and dependency).

Insee, the French institution of statistics, has emphasised the development of debt as a function of age. The slope of this curve is broadly similar everywhere, although in Anglo-Saxon countries the average level of debt is higher. As they grow older, the over 50s are wary of borrowings and bank loans. They prefer to pay cash, or to do without. It is also true that banks are sensitive to the over 50s (Figure 4.3).

Debt increases with income and relates mainly to the under 50s. There are two explanations: acquiring the main home and the commitment to enjoying life typical of the baby-boom generations. These generations have from the 1980s taken full advantage of the easy consumer credit facilities. This habit of borrowing in order to buy all kinds of goods and services will have a profound effect on the attitude of the over 50s to credit

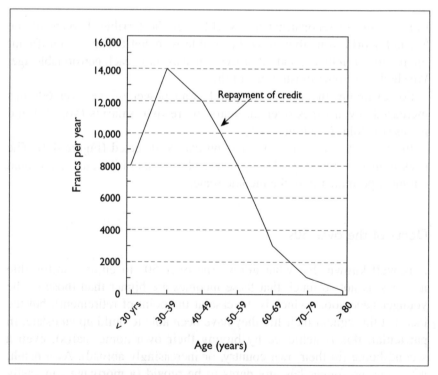

Figure 4.3 Debt according to age group

Source: Insee, Family Budget Investigation, France, 1989

in the future. The baby-boom generation will probably continue to quite an advanced age to take out loans whenever they want or need something (a trip, some new equipment). We should never forget that a generation always tends to keep its habits.

Owning property

The majority of over 50s own their own property (Table 4.2).

There is unfortunately no international comparison of the financial and property owning situations of households. As much as we have abundant and exhaustive demographic analysis, in this area we have to make approximations. It is therefore on the basis of research carried out by the different associate companies of Senioragency International that we can come up with an 'identikit' picture of the property and wealth of the over 50s in the large developed countries (USA, Japan, European Union) (Table 4.3).

Table 4.2 The property ownership of French over 50s in %

	50–54	55–59	60–64	65–69	70–74	Over 75	Total population
Owner of main home	59.2	69.7	79.6	76.2	75.7	74.6	48.7
Owner of second home	16.8	23	27	23	22.1	20.6	13.4

Source: Secodip 2000

Table 4.3 Financial strength of the over 50s in developed countries

Own their own home	70%
Own a second home	25%
Financial assets	75%
Stocks	70%
Discretionary spending power	50%
Various savings	60%
Mutual funds	Almost 40%

Source: Senioragency International, March 2002

Are all over 50s rich?

A study of the statistics reveals the phenomenal concentration of finance passing through the hands of the over 50s. However, unfortunately, by no means all of this age group benefits from such financial security. The systems in place in different countries vary and some are very unfavourable for pensioners in the labour and agricultural trades.

First, the level of pension payments remains very unequal. The result is that former managers from the public and private sectors receive on average pensions that are four to seven times higher than former agricultural managers and workers, craftsmen and retailers.

Those most susceptible to financial hardship are very old widows who have never in their lives been in salaried employment. This is clearly the case with the generations that preceded the baby boom; in those days it was normal for the wife to remain at home to keep house and bring up the children.

Some go as far as to claim that nearly half of all women pensioners live in stretched financial circumstances. So, those widows who have only part of their husband's pension to live on, depending on the country receive from 40% to 60% of the deceased's pension. All this should only prompt us to adopt a prudent and delicate approach when dealing with this market, by avoiding oversimplifications and generalisations, such as 'they are all rich'. Equally, one should avoid the trap of paying too much attention to the protestations of pensioners' associations complaining of the threat to their tax advantages in these times of economic constraint for all governments.

Their consumption

> I'm out spending my grandchildren's inheritance (US car sticker)

Where do they consume? The distribution

The received idea that the over 50s would only use local shops because they are close and suit their traditional habits is wrong. These consumers are as realistic and mobile as the rest, and the Masters and the Liberated in particular appreciate the advantages of modern distribution, such as wide choice and competitive pricing.

Table 4.4 Frequency of visits by over 50s to different retail outlets

In what type of outlet do you do most of your shopping?	First choice	% of mentions Second choice	Third choice	Total mentions
Supermarket	38.7	13.1	0.8	52.6
Traditional shop	10.6	32.0	7.8	50.4
Hypermarket	29.6	9.2	2.1	40.9
Small self-service	13.3	8.8	1.4	23.5
Market	6.3	12.0	12.0	30.3

Source: GIRA, France

Their purchases in supermarkets and hypermarkets tend to be the basic necessities. On the other hand, secondary and occasional purchases tend to favour other types of distribution, especially mail-order buying which the over 50s are skilled at. Sales of clothing to mature women through the mail has proved very successful throughout the world; this method appeals to women who often feel very rejected and even humiliated by what the fashion boutiques have to offer. In various countries, mail-order companies that have specialised in the needs of more mature women have been able to take intelligent advantage of this market by offering a very broad range of sizes, colours and fabrics that are more in tune with the tastes of such women. Another attraction of direct marketing is that it gives them time to read up on the products and services being offered.

With increasing age, visits to hypermarkets, places which tend to be cold, impersonal and remote, decline in favour of more local outlets. It is also true that retailers are mostly interested in stocking goods that appeal to young customers. Research carried out in 2000 by WSL Strategic Retail in New York under the title 'How America Shops', reported that 18–34-year-olds spend more than 20% more than they did in 1996. At the same time, the consumption of the over 60s has decreased by 9% in the same area. Is it perhaps because no one is targeting this age group? WSL asks us to take a mental walk around a shopping mall and suggest that 80% of the clothing is actually aimed at young people (Reported in the *Christian Science Monitor*, March 2001.) CREDOC has analysed visits to supermarket according to age group, as shown in Figures 4.4 and 4.5.

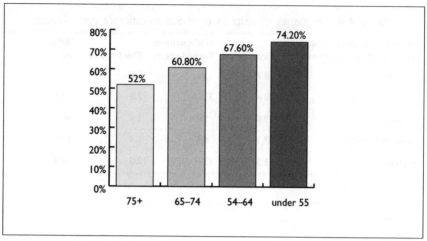

Figure 4.4 Visits to supermarkets by age group
Source: CREDOC, France

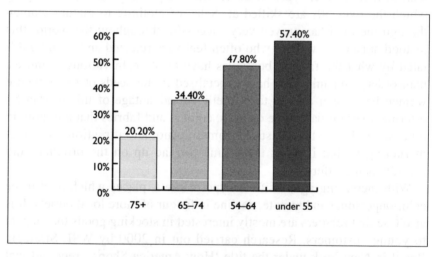

Figure 4.5 Visits to hypermarkets by age group
Source: CREDOC, France

The over 50s – the real 'Brand Victims'

It is worth repeating, since so many businesses refuse to accept it, that the over 50s are, by far, the most dedicated disciples of brands and everything they represent – quality, security, history and reputation. Proof of this can be seen in the decline in receptivity to the 'private label' brands with increasing age, and the corresponding increase in the purchase of real brands in all sectors. All the more reason for the producers not to ignore these consumers in their promotions, since they only need a little more persuasion of the right kind. The British study carried out by TGI in 1998 showed that 40% of the over 55s agreed with the statement: 'I nearly always buy well-known brands', compared with 32% of 35–54-year-olds and 25% of 16–34-year-olds.

German research conducted in September 1998 (Table 4.5) has demonstrated the growing loyalty to brands with increasing age and has also shown that with the ageing process people are also less likely to try new brands and products.

Another French study by Secodip Consoscan in 2000 (Table 4.6) shows that the consumption of retailers' own brands decreases markedly with advancing age.

Despite the importance of the over 50s in the retail turnover, a study carried out a few years ago by CECOD in France proves the lack of interest of the big name retailers in their customers over 60.

The study, which involved 800 retail outlets, showed that:

- 5.9% were in a position to establish the age of their clientele

- 5.2% judged that over 60-year-olds had particular requirements

Table 4.5 Brand loyalty and brand switching

Age groups	14–15	16–29	30–39	40–49	50–69	70+
Loyal to brands	32.3%	28.3%	32.9%	32.1%	37%	41.8%
Tries new brands	67.7%	71.7%	67.1%	67.9%	63%	58.2%

Source: GFK-Marktforschung, Omnibus-Umfrage, September 1998, Germany

Table 4.6 Retailer brands: customer distribution by buyer

	Under 35 years	35–49 years	50–64 years	65 and over
Consumers of retailer brands	23.3%	39%	21.1%	16.8%
Total consumers of retailer brands	20.7%	50.1%	19.6%	9.6%

Source: Secodip, France, 2000

- 3.4% took the needs of old people into account in their provision of goods

- 2.4% took these into account in their access arrangements

- 1% planned a study of their over 60 clientele.

A survey from Senioragency revealed that the over 60s were far from satisfied with the modern distribution outlets and criticised the selection and display of goods from many points of view (Table 4.7).

Have we really seen much progress since that study? It is doubtful. The spread of bar codes and tills equipped with optical scanners has greatly facilitated the work of the till operators as well as reducing the time spent waiting to pass through. But, apart from this, what have the hypermarket, supermarket and other popular chains done to correct the faults indicated by the over 60s?

Are the sales per square foot of a supermarket likely to be threatened by installing a few chairs or introducing some more manageable trolleys? Will making the price labels clearer and more readable affect sales to younger people? We have not mentioned the near impossibility of finding adequate toilet facilities in many stores, when it is known that there are millions of incontinent people in all countries, not to mention mothers with young children or pregnant women.

Everyone knows that there is fierce competition between modern retail distributors. Does this not present an opportunity for some organisations to give some serious thought to and implement some improvements that will appeal to this population, with its high purchasing power, that has the great virtue of loyalty, once its needs have been satisfied?

Table 4.7 Complaints of the over 60s regarding modern retail outlets

As %	60–64 years	Over 75 years
There are no seats	74.5	74.8
Too long a wait at the till	70.9	65.5
The trolleys are too awkward	29.1	36.7
The price labels are not readable	32.6	24.5
Lifts are more practical than escalators	19.9	30.9
The goods are out of reach	22.7	24.5

Source: Senioragency, 1996

VISUAL: The concept of over 60s' day –
an effective way of securing the loyalty
of this age group and stimulating sales
on a particular day

Modern American distributors have certainly come to appreciate the value of these millions of consumers with high spending power. Chains such as Sears & Roebuck, Woolworth, Hecht's Department Stores, Wal-Mart or Publix Supermarkets have embarked on ambitious training programmes for their staff, as well as refits of their stores and the creation of specific services to attract and retain this precious clientele (see visual). In the UK, 'do it yourself' specialist B&Q plc has set itself the target of having 15% of its employees aged over 50. Adding to this, the offer of a special discount of 10% for those customers over 60, on Wednesdays, has enabled the company to transform the slackest day of the week into one of the busiest. In France, some retail chains have invested in extensive marketing surveys designed to understand the needs of the over 50s better and satisfy their needs. Prominent among these are the Pinault-Printemps-Redoute group (Fnac, Conforama, Le Printemps) and the hypermarket giants Auchan or Cora. As far as the Monoprix chain is concerned, it is very strongly established in town centres, has considerably increased the size of its price labels, refined its range of products and extended its services, such as home delivery. Boulanger (Auchan group), the electronics and white goods supplier, has been the first to test the American concept of over 50s day, by creating the 'Boulanger Senior Tuesday', with preferential treatment for this group on arrival, free tuition with multimedia purchases, goods transported to the vehicle, and so on.

Three factors explaining the consumer behaviour of the over 50s

■ *Age effect*

A person's age influences their needs. Their state of health rules out certain types of goods and services in favour of others. Whether one accepts or rejects the idea of growing older, at around 45 nearly everyone becomes long-sighted and has to resort to reading glasses or contact lenses. At 60, hearing difficulties emerge; at 85, 25% of men and 40% of women are incontinent, and so on.

■ *Generation effect*

To belong to a generation means having a history and consumption habits acquired during childhood and adulthood. These appear pronounced in the new over 50s since 1996 who came from the baby boom and who throughout their lives have shown a strong tendency to (over-) consume and whose lifestyle has always been to enjoy themselves.

■ *Effect of the present*

This is the effect that the contemporary environment has on the habits of the over 50s. If it comes up to their expectations, modernity interests them as much as it interests the younger age groups that are completely open to new goods and services. But the over 50s have greater demands as to quality; they steer clear of pointless and shoddy gadgets and prefer solid value.

Their strength in various markets

Let us take the example of the European Union, where it is estimated that between 1977 and 1997 consumption by the over 50s increased by 64% compared with an average of 22% for the rest of the population. This goes to show that we are dealing with a target market of consumers with high potential. In the UK, this was quantified by the ONS Family Spending Survey in 1996 that showed an average weekly expenditure per person of £114.86 for those aged 30–49, £143.20 between 50–64, £117.76 between 65–74, and £95.83 for the over 75s. A study in Japan carried out in 2000 by Dentsu showed that the over 50s have become bigger consumers than the younger generations (Figure 4.6).

Space does not permit an exhaustive analysis of all markets to establish the share held by the over 50s. We shall therefore examine some examples from quite different sectors. Because there is no official information source, governmental or private, that has analysed internationally the consumption

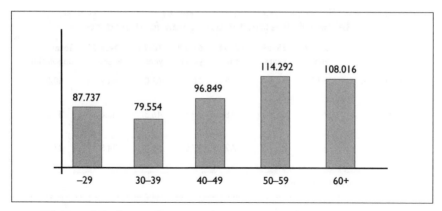

Figure 4.6 Rate of consumption per month/per person (yen) in Japan (national average 99,150 yen per month)
Source: Dentsu, 2000

level of the over 50s in the markets for goods, equipment and services, we have, through the different parts of Senioragency International, put together our own collection of data from hundreds of sources, panels and studies from around the world. This enables us to establish the high level of consistency in the consumption of the over 50s in 2000. The summaries of the results are valid everywhere, to within a few per cent.

The over 50s and food

There are four key parameters that determine the behaviour of the over 50s so far as food is concerned.

Health and figure

Looking after one's diet is a basic requirement for a better and healthier quality of life into old age. In their concern for a healthier, more varied and balanced diet, the over 50s go for lower-fat products and foods that will help sustain their 'health capital'. A study carried out by the French dairy industry has also shown that 86% of those aged 50–64 claim to be ready to pay more for quality, 70.9% say they intend to eat more 'bio' products in future and 81.8% say they have changed to lower-fat products (CIDIL Observer 1998, France).

Table 4.8 Reasons for buying new food products							
	50–54 years	55–59 years	60–64 years	67–69 years	70–74 years	Over 75 years	Total population
In the interests of my health	52.2	56.5	62.9	58.6	63.0	64.1	50.5
In order to remain fit	46.7	45.4	49.8	49.1	46.3	46.6	41.2
To try new products	33.5	33.1	27.2	27.9	26.2	24.8	37.8

Source: Secodip Simm 1999, France

Skills and their transmission to the younger generations

People living as a couple take pleasure in preparing a meal together. They feel that they are practising a skill. They like passing this knowledge on to their children and grandchildren at Sunday lunches and other occasions that bring the family together.

Pleasure above all

The over 50s want to enjoy life while not going without the pleasure of eating well, as far as possible. Torn between this desire and the concern to preserve their health, they find a middle way by avoiding excess. The idea of low-fat products is the complete answer to this problem (Table 4.8).

A preference for fresh products

The over 50s consume more fresh produce than the whole of the population.

Fresh and natural products allow them to enjoy and practice their culinary skills while consuming foods that are full of vitamins. They spend the most (in absolute value) in the food sector (Table 4.9).

Table 4.9 Examples of the over 50s' market share in different classes of food (estimated average for large developed countries)

Breakfast	Percentage in value of over 50s households in 2000	Liquids	Percentage in value of over 50s households in 2000
Soluble coffee	59	Wine	62
Jam	57	Champagne	55
Honey	55	Whisky	52
Tea	53	Carbonated water	51
Bread/biscuits	51	Still water	49
Ground coffee	51	Beer	43
Cereals	24	Fruit juices and nectars	36

Dishes	Percentage in value of over 50s households in 2000	Culinary aids	Percentage in value of over 50s households in 2000
Fresh fish	67	Sweeteners	61
Seafood	66	Olive oil	61
Fresh meat	54	Vinegar	59
Poultry	49	Sugar	53
Raw ham	47	Pepper, spices	47
Tinned fish	43	Vinaigrettes, sauces for salads	41
Suzimi, taramasalata, eggs, fish	42		

Source: Senioragency International, 2000

The over 50s and insurance

Insurance companies take the credit for being the first to appreciate the considerable potential presented by the needs of the over 50s. Almost all insurance companies have launched promotions aimed at the older generations; some, such as the British Norwich Union, have been active in this sphere for a very long time. With advancing age, people's feeling of insecurity grows, one has more possessions, one is continually anxious about the future; the conditions are right to take out a number of insurance policies.

We draw attention to two insurance markets that should be important in the future: health insurance against illnesses likely to result in a high level of dependence and funeral insurance.

Dependency insurance (also called long-term care insurance) allows people to protect themselves against the considerable financial risks of becoming dependent on care, such costs not being borne by the state social security or the complementary mutual insurance societies. If the person's pension is insufficient to cover this sum, it will fall to the family to make up the difference. Given the spectacular increase in life expectancy and the build up in numbers of this population, long-term care insurance will certainly become a basic choice for the insurance portfolio of the over 50s (see visual).

VISUAL: Direct Line was one of the first insurance companies in Europe to target 50+, eight years ago

Another insurance contract whose future seems bright is funeral insurance. More and more pensioners are keen to ensure that everything is organised and prepaid, in order to avoid any additional burden on their family at the time of their death.

The over 50s and car ownership; nearly one in two new cars

It is well known that car manufacturers are not interested in the over 50s. However, a few months after Renault launched the Twingo in France, a small car available in all colours and with frog's eyes, the average age of buyers had risen to 48. The amazing fact was that between a quarter and a third of buyers were over 50. The marketing executives at Renault who had in no sense anticipated this infatuation tried for several weeks to cover up the sales figures, presumably fearing that this would create a negative image for their new baby. Since then, somewhat gingerly, manufacturers have begun to integrate this target market in the design of their vehicles, but not in their advertising.

Essentially then, the car is a typical product for the over 50s. All the more so because they buy:

■ new, rather than second hand

■ top of the range, with all the extras.

It can be reckoned generally that more or less everywhere in the developed countries the over 50s make up about 50% of the market for new cars and about 70% of the top of the range market. As an illustration we shall look at two large European markets, the UK and France (Tables 4.10, 4.11 and 4.12).

Table 4.10 The UK car market – who buys?				
Age	1987	1990	1995	2000
17–29	12%	12%	13%	14%
30–44	36%	32%	28%	25%
45–59	31%	29%	32%	31%
60+	22%	26%	27%	30%
Source: Ford UK 2001				

Table 4.11 Purchase of new cars in France by the over 50s between 1991 and 1993		
Models	Total %	% of over 50s
Under 2CV	−10.0	−3.8
Under 4CV	−6.3	−4.9
5/7 CV	+5.3	+3.4
8/9 CV	−8.8	+10.3
Over 10 CV	0	+23.5
Source: Simm 1995, France		

Table 4.12 Reasons for car purchase					
Under 50 years		50–65 years		Over 65 years	
Style	31%	Loyalty	38%	Loyalty	48%
Loyalty	22%	Style	22%	Style	13%
Price	20%	Reliability	17%	Reliability	13%
Equipment	17%	Price	14%	Price	10%
Reliability	17%	Equipment	10%	Compact size	9%
Source: Ford (UK) 2001					

According to Renault, in 1996, one customer in two was over 50 and one in three over 60. They accounted for:

- 46% of the luxury and sport car market
- 40% of the top of the range market
- 47% of the upper mid-range market
- 42% of the lower mid-range market
- 35% of the small car market
- 41% of the economy car market.

As an aside, we would mention that the average age of buyers of Harley-Davidson motorcycles is 52 – a detail that may alter somewhat the image of the Harley's usual rider!

The over 50s and domestic equipment and electronic leisure goods

The equipment level of the 50–59 age group is always above average, whether we are talking about refrigerator, freezer, washing machine, dishwasher, vacuum cleaner, sewing machine or colour TV and video recorder (Table 4.13).

As for those over 60, who have only been retired for a short time, the growth in such equipment has been even greater.

Who has decreed that to sell a meat roaster or an electric cafetière one needs to target the under 50s? More than other age groups, the over 50s attach high priority to their quality of life.

But, if they already have equipment, why try to sell them more? In outline, the over 50s have adopted high lifestyle values; to spend is to improve one's life. In this respect they are totally at odds with the under 40s who want to reduce their expenditure owing to the economic conditions, in order to pay for their house, for example.

We are witnessing a renewal phase in equipment and furniture, where the over 50s are refitting their interiors with high quality goods at the time when their children are leaving the nest. For example, for several years the new fitted kitchen market has been dominated largely by over 50s couples.

Table 4.13 Average equipment level for the Masters

Product	Total population	50–59 years
Dishwasher	40%	55%
Colour TV	95%	97%
Video recorder	72%	78%
Freezer	57%	68%
Microwave oven	59%	64%
Personal computer	21%	24%

Source: Senioragency International, estimated average for developed countries in 2000

The over 50s and cosmetics

If there is one area where the myth of eternal youth holds sway it is that of cosmetics and beauty products. Marketing executives cling fast to the belief that women do not want to see themselves growing older and therefore this youth must be promised to them through images of beautiful young models. This type of promotion is certainly very effective among young women, but how is it possible to imagine that the millions of older women, who consume and over consume quantities of cosmetic products, will be able to recognise themselves in the form of a 20-year-old who could be their grand-daughter? Women over 50, even less than others, do not expect some anti-ageing miracle; they are simply looking for some real feel-good sensation and an effective means of delaying the effects of ageing. Table 4.14 shows the level of use of some beauty products.

In this context, the Nivea Vital campaign, launched in 1994 was truly revolutionary (see visual). For the first time, a brand dared to present a

VISUAL: The European launch of Nivea Vital stimulated the marketing community. Thanks to this, things have changed!

Table 4.14 Level of use of products

Types of product	Under 50 years	Over 50 years
Face cream	68.1%	77.9%
Hair colourant	40.0%	74.0%
Cream	56.8%	61.9%
Anti-wrinkle cream	14.6%	25.4%
Source: Senioragency International		

model of 52 with grey hair and attractive wrinkles. Suzanne Schöneborn immediately became a worldwide celebrity among over 50s women who were able to identify with this credible spokeswoman who told them about natural skin-care products.

This campaign opened the door to a number of other brands that began to adopt more realistic methods of conveying their message. An example

VISUAL: L'Oréal benefited from the help of the
beautiful 50-year-old Dayle Haddon

VISUAL: Novadiol Italy made a very
'upfront' ad aimed at mature women

is L'Oréal (see visual), who in 2001 launched its new product for mature skins, 'Age Perfect', with the attractive 50-year-old Dayle Haddon, or Estée Lauder, who for its 'Resilience Lift' range had the idea of using its former star model Karen Graham for a world launch in 2000. The same woman, 30 years later, still as beautiful, but with maturity as well. Here we have three striking examples of how the canons of beauty are coming in step with the reality of our society.

It is estimated that one pot of face cream in two is bought by a woman of over 50, and that, on average, such a woman spends two hours a day in her bathroom, compared with 20 minutes for a woman of 20!

Here are some significant details:

- 71% of women over 50 use lipstick (37% of the market)

- 44% use foundation creams (36% of the market)

■ 81% use face creams (53% of the market)

■ 51% apply nail varnish (36% of the market).

(Senioragency International, average for developed countries 2000)

The over 50s and telecommunications

If the over 50s use the telephone more often than others, it is to keep in close contact with the family and therefore overcome loneliness. While they are already well equipped, they are destined to become a choice target for the communications companies (Table 4.15).

The Masters (50–59 years) in particular are a group who when working will have had mobile telephones with amplifiers and number storage.

At the moment, very few operators or manufacturers of mobile telephones have attempted cornering the fabulous market potential of the over 50s. The main thrust of the industry in all countries continues to be focused on the young and active. However, the security aspect of the mobile is a strong argument for this market, which is itself becoming increasingly mobile. Again, it should be stressed that the design and ergonomics of the handsets need to suit their sight (long-sightedness being the norm for the over 50s) and their less precise touch after 65 (arthritis). One exception that should be mentioned is the Japanese mobile giant NTT Do Co Mo that launched a new model in 2001 called 'RAKU-RAKU' (Raku means easy and comfortable in Japanese) which has three direct buttons, large letters, an easy to read panel and an easier menu of functions.

Table 4.15 Levels of telephone ownership	
Set of households	93.6
60–64 years	94.4
65–69 years	96.3
70–74 years	94.4
75–79 years	94.4
Source: CERC, France	

The over 50s and tourism

The age of maturity is also the golden age of leisure. With the children now independent, family constraints are fewer in number. It is the time when one benefits from the possibilities of accrued wealth and has a strong urge to make up for lost time.

The pensioner is a preferred consumer; he or she can travel throughout the year and at attractive rates.

The over 50s already amount to 33% of the European travel market (the equivalent of 300 million journeys) and 37% of the organised holiday market.

Today, although fewer of them go on holiday during the holiday period, they go away more. The over 65s on average take 33 days, compared with 28 days for the total population.

One has only to visit airports or main line stations to see how strongly the over 50s are represented in the travelling public. And these are not holidaymakers just seeking the beach. Table 4.16 shows the main reasons for travelling. An original travel agency launched in 1997 in the suburbs of Washington, called 'Grandtravel', has specialised in the arrangement of trips to bring grandparents and grandchildren together. One of the packages that has enjoyed great success is called 'Patriotic Panorama' and involves an eight-day trip visiting the famous places in the history of the USA. It offers a means for the older generation to pass on the cultural heritage to their grandchildren.

Also worth mentioning is the extraordinary success in the UK of the Saga Group, started in 1951, in Folkestone, by Sydney De Haan, then owner of a small hotel in the town. Noticing how short the tourist season was in that area, he had the idea of attracting British pensioners, who were available all year round looking for peace and quiet, and who would appreciate the lower off-season rates since many had only quite modest

Table 4.16 The motivation to travel		
	50–64 years	**Over 65 years**
Discover a new culture	57.2%	47.6%
Visit museums	15.7%	18.7%
Meet people	31.3%	28.8%
Attend an event	1.7%	2.4%
Source: Simm, France		

Elle est pas belle la vie ?

NOUVELLE
CARTE
SENIOR
LE TRAIN À -50%*
+5 SERVICES
À PRIX RÉDUIT

Vous avez 60 ans et plus ! Profitez des nouveaux services que vous réserve la Carte Senior de la SNCF ! Toute l'année, vous bénéficiez de 50 %* de réduction sur la majorité des trains (et –25 % garantis dans tous les cas*).

Mais désormais, la Carte Senior vous offre également des réductions permanentes sur 5 services dédiés au plaisir de voyager : le Service Bagages à domicile, la restauration à bord, la location de voitures, les nuits d'hôtel et la traversée pour la Corse. Alors, elle est pas belle la vie ?

*OFFRES PERMANENTES. Soumises à conditions. Renseignez-vous en gare, boutiques SNCF ou agences de voyages agréées, ou par Ligne Directe au 08 36 35 35 35 (2,21F/min – 0,34 €). Voir conditions d'utilisation dans le livret de présentation Carte Senior envoyé à votre domicile environ un mois après l'achat de la carte. Offre Service Bagages à domicile disponible à partir du 01/07/01.

voyages-sncf.com

AVIS

SNCF

VISUAL: SNCF — the French railways have very successfully developed a new 'Senior Card' using a very positive slogan: 'Isn't life wonderful?'

pensions. He was a true pioneer, for in the 1950s, people were even less interested in the over 50s than now. His initiative was quickly successful and his small hotel became fully booked, so his next idea was to suggest his scheme to fellow hoteliers along the coast. From the 1960s, Saga began to offer holidays outside the UK, offering the air and cruise operators the opportunity of filling their off-peak seasons with British pensioners. Since then the development of Saga has seen it occupy new sectors of the market. Today, the Saga Group has a turnover of 500 million euros, 1.1 million household customers and a database holding 33% of the over 50s in the UK. In order to promote all these new products and services, the monthly *Saga Magazine* was launched and has become the leading publication in the field with 1.1 million copies. The company now

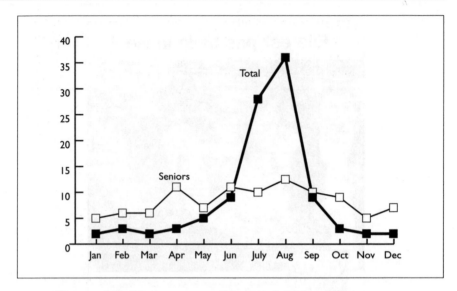

Figure 4.7 European over 50s travel in their own country,
compared with the total travel in the market

Source: ETC

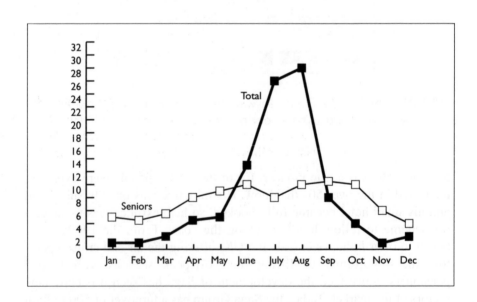

Figure 4.8 European over 50s travel abroad,
compared with the total travel in the market

Source: ETC

Your Grandkids Already Adore You.

Call For This Free Video, Anyhow.

Imagine what a grand time you'd have with your grandkids at the most magical place on earth. This free *Walt Disney World* vacation planning video will show you where to stay, what to do, how to spend less time in line and have a ball together. So call for your free video. But only if you can handle more bear hugs and sticky kisses.

Call 1-800-515-2692 today.

Please respond by 6/30/01.
Allow 2-3 weeks for your free video to arrive.
Must be 18 or older to receive video.
©Disney

Walt Disney World.
disneyworld.com

VISUAL: Walt Disney identified long ago that 50+ were also grandparents
Source: © Disney Enterprises, Inc

operates in all fields of interest to the over 50s (insurance, investment, car purchase). To quote Tim Bull, planning director of Saga:

> Travel is Saga's Trojan Horse; customers will let us in more readily to find out about travel, and often our other services will be hiding inside the magazine. Sadly, financial services on their own are just not fun for customers.

A French comment illustrates the radical change in the tastes of the over 50s over the years:

> At the beginning, it offered the possibility of travel to people who were quite unassuming. Some had never seen the sea. Today, our customers of over 55 have already travelled. They are harder to please in terms of hotel accommodation, trips, and so on.

This was the view of Mrs Guerbé, of the Federation of Clubs for the Rural Elderly of Calvados, that now offers trips to far-off destinations, such as Thailand, Florida, Norway and Canada.

The fact that former agricultural workers supposedly so home-loving, can have such requirements shows how the attitude of the over 50s has changed spectacularly in a few decades.

For the future, one can predict phenomenal growth in over 50s tourism with the retirement of the baby boomers who have always been active and curious. The Yankelovitch Monitor carried out a survey in 2000 which showed that 90% of the baby boomers say that they will travel more as soon as the children have moved out.

CHAPTER 5

Abolishing preconceptions

From the age of 40 a man is called an old man. Old men are suspicious, jealous, mean, gloomy, talkative, always complaining, they are incapable of friendship
FROM *RICHELET DICTIONARY*, 1679

It is difficult to struggle against preconceptions and stereotypes. The over 50s are a prime target for both. The expression itself conjures up a wall of prejudice.

Fortunately, the images that are continually applied to them are in the process of changing. The press is playing a positive role in their rehabilitation. We are pleased to find that there is an active, sporting and even romantic life the other side of the fateful 50 years marker.

Things are moving. As the redoubtable creator of fashion and public opinion, the press has seized upon the topic. Its support will facilitate a better understanding of this population that has been so neglected, misunderstood and sometimes denigrated. Many journalists have 'fallen in love' with the over 50s.

To quote the British journalist Rachel Miller:

> In the world of advertising, the over 50s have their place. They drink tea but never touch soft drinks, don't eat crisps or chocolate, don't shave and therefore have no need for aftershave, but they're pretty good at calling their friends and family!

Or again, Raymond Snoddy, media editor of *The Times*:

> Less than 10% of the UK advertising campaigns' expenditure is directed at consumers over 50. If there is a rational argument that justifies applying only 10% of spending to an annual pile of loot of £166 billion, it would be good to hear it!

Let us take advantage of this new interest to do away with some of the false ideas that have blurred the perception of advertising and promotion executives concerning the over 50s.

The US survey company, Donneley Marketing, measured the differences between the idea that marketing managers had about the over 50s' behaviours and interests and what that group actually said about themselves. This survey showed the gulf between them.

We see the typical view of the supposed indifference of the over 50s towards new brands and products (we shall examine this later).

Question: What are the products and services that are of most interest to the over 50s?
Response in Table 5.1.1

Question: Which is the preferred means for the over 50s to discover a product or service?
Response in Table 5.1.2

Table 5.1 The over 50s as they see themselves and as they are seen by marketing managers

1 Products and services

Product or service	Replies of the over 50s	Marketing managers
Cars	3.1	2.9
Education, culture	3.1	2.9
Financial services	3.7	4.3
Care, health	4.1	4.7
Travel	3.6	4.2

(In order of importance, on a scale of 1 to 5, with 5 as maximum)

2 The route to the discovery of a new product

Means	Replies of the over 50s	Marketing managers
Direct marketing	2.3	3.0
Magazines	2.3	3.3
Word of mouth	3.6	4.3
TV or radio	2.3	3.0
Trying a new brand	3.5	3.0
Trying a new product	3.6	3.0

(In order of importance, on a scale of 1 to 5, with 5 as maximum)
Source: Donneley Marketing

Table 5.2 Increasingly hedonistic behaviour		
Persons over 60 approving the statement		
	Germany	France
'Instead of economising all one's life, one should use one's money to make life pleasant'	53%	64%
Source: JWGU and Senioragency		

Several recent studies, one carried out by the German institute JWGU and another by Senioragency on 522 over 50s in June 1996 focused on the attitude to consumption of those over 60 (Table 5.2). They reveal a growing pursuit of pleasure and an unbounded desire to enjoy life. This sensual aspect is bound to surprise a marketing manager convinced that only the young indulge themselves.

The European institute IPSOS published in December 2000 a survey carried out in the European Union on behalf of the credit organisation SOFINCO concerning the over 50s. The researchers noted the pleasure-seeking characteristic of this group. Asked to choose between 'spending one's money in order to enjoy life' or 'keeping it to pass on to their family', a majority of the over 50s opted for the first, without hesitation. The most determined to do this were the Dutch 73%, followed by the British 69%, the Germans 64%, the Belgians 53% and the French 50%.

In Japan, Dentsu compared the attitude of the over 50s between 1999 and 1992 on a number of criteria. The researchers were struck by the modifications to the traditional Japanese attitudes with regard to the children of the over 50s.

> Changes have taken place in terms of people's relationship with their children, as exemplified by the seven-point decline from 57% to 50% in the number of respondents who agreed with the statement, 'I want to leave an inheritance for my children.' The number of people wanting to spend their old age living with their children also declined from 65% to 54%. (Yuko Wada in Dentsu Japan 2001 Marketing and Advertising Yearbook)

If one analyses the most current preconceptions, one realises that these errors in perception arise rather from a failure to recognise the attitudes and behaviour of the over 50s than from a systematic desire to denigrate.

First preconception – the over 50s feel old

It takes a long time to become young (Pablo Picasso)

A pavement video caught the live reactions of over 50s to all kinds of subject and types of product. One of the questions concerned the age of the interviewee and in particular the age that he/she 'felt'. The results were spectacular. Almost unanimously, those questioned stated that they felt themselves to be 10 to 15 years younger. This is one of the best known phenomena of over 50s marketing; the psychological or cognitive age, one's own perception of one's age, is more important than the physiological age, as illustrated in Figure 5.1.

In the majority of cases, the over 50s subtract 10 to 20 years from their real age. This is quite natural because they feel fit and in control of their faculties, physical and intellectual. It is interesting to note that two groups of very different age, young children and the over 50s, have this tendency to disassociate their real age from their desired age. The children want to be older than ten to be able to do the marvellous things that grown-ups can do, while the over 50s do not see the ravages of time on their bodies. This is an interesting duality of personality that is crucial for marketing and advertising.

It is therefore necessary to pay great attention to the actors and models used in TV and press campaigns to ensure that they convey the best image of 'eternal youth'. This does not mean that young 50s performers should be systematically featured, but those that have a 'young image'. It does not matter if they are 80, as long as their 80 years are filled with positive attributes: health, fitness, internal youth (a very famous Nike advertisement in the US starred a centenarian baseball player).

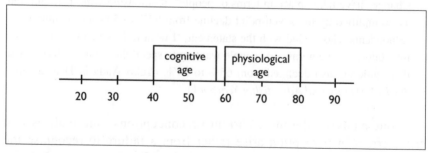

Figure 5.1 Gap between physiological age and cognitive age

Source: Senioragency

Table 5.3 Real age and perceived age	
You have told me you are aged 60 or more. Would you say that you feel closer to someone who is aged ...	Replies (%)
Under 30 years	12
Between 30 and 40 years	15
Between 41 and 50 years	18
Between 51 and 60 years	18
Between 61 and 70 years	19
Over 70 years	8
No opinion	10
Source: IFOP, sample of 567 over 60s, France	

In France, IFOP have measured the extent of this phenomenon in a survey that allowed an evaluation of the divergence between real age and perceived age (Table 5.3).

Some Liberated and Peaceful say they feel younger than 30 years! Summing the first three lines of Table 5.3 we have 45% respondents who feel that they are 50, or even less. They therefore give themselves ten years less than their true age. In a research study carried out by the Japanese cosmetic group Shiseido in September 2000, Japanese women over 50 were asked their age and what age they felt they were. On average, women aged 60–64 felt their age to be 52.7 years, that is, 9.1 years younger, and those aged 65–70 felt their age to be 57.9 years, 8.9 years younger. A survey made by Sofres for the IPSEN institute in June 1995 using a sample of 5000 people over 60 showed that 74% of them felt 'young' or 'quite young', and 2.3% 'very young'!

An American study (by *US News and World Report*) revealed how adults, at different stages in their life, defined 'being old'. Among young adults, 21% asserted that one is old after 50, and 27% said after 60. On the other hand, 33% of those aged 45–54 thought that one is old after 70. In the 65 and over group, one-third of people said one is old after 80! The older one grows, the further one pushes the definition of old age. To quote the famous remark of Bernard Baruch, US statesman, who when aged 90 stated: 'Old age is always 15 years on from where you are.'

Second preconception – they are physically and socially inactive

The word inactive is itself offensive. It conjures up the image of a wheel-chair or an armchair fixed in front of the TV. This erroneous picture needs to be attacked and some less degrading terminology adopted.

The legs …

The French State Secretariat for Youth and Sport published the top favourite activities of those over 65. These were:

1. Walking   30%

2. Physical exercise   19%

3. Swimming   10%

Still in France, in 2000 32.1% of women over 65 and 38.8% of men of the same age claimed to participate regularly or occasionally in some kind of sporting activity. This shows spectacular progress, for in 1967, a similar INSEE investigation showed that 8% of the over 65s were active in sport. The study of the French Committee for Health Education (CFES) in 2000 showed that the levels of sporting activity of the over 50s was very comp-arable with those of the younger generations (see Table 5.4).

Table 5.4 Sporting activity during the past week		
Age (years)	Men %	Women %
12–14	89.5	82.7
15–19	75.6	67.2
20–25	57.7	35.1
26–34	45.4	33.0
35–44	44.9	35.6
45–54	35.3	32.5
55–64	35.5	35.0
65–75	32.7	26.9
Source: CFES, 2000		

Sports	Millions active aged over 55	Percentage of over 55s in relation to total practising the sport
Table 5.5 Over 55s and sport in the USA		
Walking	16.0	27.4
Fishing	6.7	14.6
Swimming	6.2	9.4
Bowling	6.2	15.4
Cruising, sailing	5.5	17.8
Cycling	4.9	9.2
Gymnastics	3.8	11.0
Golf	3.6	17.8

Source: National Sporting Goods Association

These studies illustrate the pronounced change in the over 50s. Imagine the further changes, now that the baby-boom generation, brought up on jogging and tennis, are coming to form the ranks of the Masters.

The cupboards of the over 50s now contain Nike or Reebok trainers rather than orthopaedic shoes or slippers. Jane Fonda and her cohort of admirers have a good future ahead. The over 50s want to feel good in themselves; they know that taking part in some sporting activity helps this feeling of well being.

In the USA, the National Sporting Goods Association has for many years studied the sports behaviour of the over 55s. It has established that 31% of this group are regular walkers and many practise other sporting activities. Table 5.5 shows the breakdown of their activities.

One scarcely needs to remark how interesting these figures are to the manufacturers of sports equipment, especially when we recall how keen the over 55s are on quality goods and how they favour brand names.

With their customary dynamism, US advertisers quickly launched and sponsored Senior Olympic Games, Masters Tennis Programs and other Senior Gold Tours throughout the USA.

In 2001, in France, the insurance group AGF-Allianz in association with the Internet site seniorplanet.fr, launched the first over 50s national tennis tournament, which proved very successful.

In the 1993 New York Marathon, all the TV cameras followed the exploits of Mavis Lindgren who took part for the third time in the most famous marathon in the world. Why such interest in a sportswoman who won no prizes? Quite simply, because she was aged 86, had begun her marathon 'career' at the age of 62, in response to several angina attacks and had already taken part in some 70 marathon runs. She described her new life in a stimulating best-seller called *Grandma wears running shoes*. This was a fine example for all over 50s, and those much younger.

... and the head

What would become of the museums, historic buildings and exhibitions without the over 50s? They represent 28% of the visits paid to historic buildings and since 1967 their visits to museums have increased threefold. Every year, throughout the world, many of them enrol on university courses to gain knowledge that has hitherto been too difficult to acquire. Some 75% believe that it is right time in their life to extend themselves intellectually.

This is one of the many reasons that explains their infatuation with the Internet, which is for them a bottomless well of knowledge that allows them to indulge in their many hobbies and interests (genealogy, art history, tours of virtual museums, gardens, and so on).

A very active associative life

The word 'active' is a key to what many over 50s seek to be, since they often have the impression of having been excluded from their 'activity' by an imposed retirement, leaving them with a feeling of social and economic uselessness. An associative and cultural life, and voluntary work, are powerful outlets for an intellectual curiosity that is often robust.

When visiting towns in the USA that have been much developed over the past 30 years, based on the Sun City concept, that is, reserved for couples where at least one member is over 55, one is struck by the importance of the civic tasks carried out by the inhabitants themselves, strictly on the basis of free voluntary service. This includes policing and street cleaning for towns of 50, 000 inhabitants!

There are many examples of this powerful urge that drives pensioners to make themselves useful, to help others, in order to find a social role that was taken away from them by the abruptness of their retirement.

The figures for active participation in associations among the over 50s, especially pensioners, are more or less similar in the USA, the EU and Japan and are shown in Table 5.6. Around 40–45% of the over 55s lead an

Table 5.6 Percentage participation by those aged 40+ in all types of association, club or other organisation in developed countries		
Age	Women	Men
40–59 years	43%	54%
60 years and over	36%	44%
Source: Senioragency International		

associative life. Some of these associations may be very professional and specific; in France, for example, there is the EGEE association which helps businesses that have an exact and specific problem by allocating to them on a voluntary basis retired people who have the required expertise. The ECTI association operates in France and abroad with small and medium-sized businesses, and the AGIR association sends over 55s from all fields (craftsmen, educators and engineers) into developing countries and into Eastern countries. Or again, there is the Federation of Rural Elders, which has some 900,000 members and works actively for preservation and regeneration of the rural environment.

Some associations are particularly stimulating. The 'Panthères Grises', formed all over the world and based on the American Gray Panthers, has been described by its French delegate as 'a band of women who have decided to use old age in the most creative way possible ... We are the itchy skin of the over 60s and the politicians.' Some of the aims of these pensioners (excluding men) is to change the attitude of businesses and communities towards the over 50s and to urge them, for example, to call upon retired people when colleagues have an ill child, or to create local houses where pensioners could come to help children with their school work. Inter-generation solidarity is something that the over 50s are keen to promote.

Well in advance of his time, Gilbert Trigano saw the advantage to Club Méditerranée of enrolling 'Kind Grannies' to look after the very young children in the Baby Clubs at the different sites. This was a clever way to reassure the parents and children, as well as sending a positive message to the over 50s that they were appreciated and welcomed at Club Med.

One of these new style 'Kind Grannies', Michèle Hourquin, gave her views:

On my return to Paris, my friends found me rejuvenated. In fact, I am less lonely because I feel that I am useful, I am exploiting my potential and putting it to good use in a pleasant environment and not in an office. Although my work is voluntary, it enriches in another way and profoundly. (*Enfants Magazine*)

Renault, too, came up with a great innovation when they launched the Renault Ambassadors Club to bring together the 85,000 pensioners of the company. It is a well known fact that many former employees retain a strong attachment to their old company. This is especially so in the car industry and with Renault it is said that many of their pensioners have a 'diamond badge' (the Renault logo) instead of a heart!

Renault realised that they could make good use of these pensioners to increase sales of their cars by allowing them the facility of being able to buy several new vehicles each year to be resold by these 'ambassadors' to family members and relations. To give some idea of the importance of this initiative, Renault sells on average some 15,000 cars per year to its pensioners, more than half of which go to 'ambassadors' who are truly active and who only amount to some 25% of the total number of pensioners. Some of them have even sold, or caused to be sold through their influence on dealers, as many as six vehicles a year. This is a clever example of how to recreate links between a business and its former employees, while at the same time being an astute commercial move.

Third preconception – their health is bad

The further ages advances, the greater the potential threat to health; this is only normal. On the other hand, no one would contest that to put all the over 50s in the same bag and imagine that they are in a bad way is false. We all know people of 70 or even 80 in our circle who are full of energy and vitality and bear no resemblance to the conventional imagery of the 'old man' crippled with rheumatism and even more dreadful illnesses. Of course, we concede that 'ageing is an inherited disease' that attacks the body in a number of places. The skin becomes thinner and loses its suppleness, one becomes breathless easily, bones become more fragile, sight declines, colours become confused, cataracts threaten, hearing alters with higher frequency sounds being lost, arthritis deforms the fingers and wrists making movements painful and less precise, impotency and incontinency become serious issues ...

Not everyone is affected by these different phenomena at the same age, nor at the same rate or with the same intensity (Table 5.7). A body that has been well fed and well looked after will only decline slowly, whereas one that has had to put up with excessive weight, stress, different accidents,

Table 5.7 Leading chronic conditions at 65 and over in the USA	
Disease	Prevalence %
Arthritis	50.2
Hypertension	36.4
Heart disease	32.5
Hearing impairment	28.6
Cataracts	16.6
Deformity or orthopaedic impairment	16.6
Chronic sinusitis	15.1
Diabetes	10.1
Tinnitus	9.0

Source: American Cancer Society 1997

tobacco and alcohol, runs the risk of degrading at an amazing speed and certainly sooner.

For many, failing health appears only through a few discomforts and little difficulties.

As part of a study made in February 1994 using a national sample of people aged 60 and over, the French institute, IFOP, produced an index of activities that become more difficult with increasing age. These are in order of importance:

- Going up and down stairs
- Sewing or threading a needle
- Reaching objects placed high up
- Following a conversation involving several people
- Reading price labels in shops
- Carrying shopping home.

The Gallup Institute in the USA carried out a similar study. Its results helped many American companies to improve their products to make them simpler to use and more accessible. One of the best known examples involves the packaging of a medicine commonly sold in the USA, called Tylenol. This painkiller is used instead of aspirin by the majority of Americans and sells in huge quantities (see visual).

VISUAL: Tylenol has for many years targeted mature people with very efficient ads

For safety reasons, the container had for many years a cap that opened when one pressed on it vertically if the cap was correctly positioned in front of a tiny arrow. This is a tricky manoeuvre for anyone and a real nightmare for the elderly. After two years of research and tests, a new cap was introduced. This work earned the company the US Oscar for product design for the over 50s in 1993 and resulted in greatly increased sales of the drug.

Other companies are beginning to pay attention to the specific needs of the over 50s. For example, there are the publishers that produce series of books in large print. Panasonic revolutionised the microwave oven market with its Dimension 4 machine. Instead of the two dials for heating level and cooking time (that required calculations before cooking a dish), this oven had a series of buttons, very clearly marked with pictures of the most

VISUAL: Peugeot cycle: you can get the same
comfort from your cycle as your car!

common dishes; the machine did the rest. For some years, Peugeot cycles
have promoted the Senior Cycle. Their City 805 model has comfortable
shock absorbers front and rear, ergonomic and comfortable saddle, 21
gears controlled by twist grip, halogen lighting – a cycle that yields
nothing to a car! (See visual).

For their part, Yamaha have developed a cycle fitted with an electric
motor which cuts in automatically (or when switched on manually) as
soon as the rider encounters an upward slope. This is a perfect product for
those over 50s who want to practise a sport while having some physical
assistance available if needed.

AT&T brought out a range of telephones with large buttons that were a
great success. In France, two telephones from France Telecom have been
produced to facilitate use by disabled and elderly people: they are the
'Celesta 250' and the 'Amifil'. Scrabble introduced a set of their game
with larger, more readable tiles.

In Japan, as already mentioned, NTT Do Co Mo has recently brought
out a mobile model ideally suited to mature users. It has easy-to-call
buttons connected to children or police or doctor and a more readable
panel for 'older eyes' (see visual).

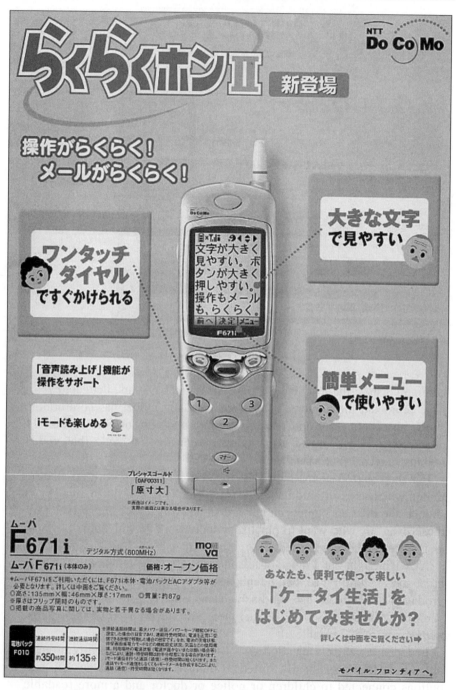

VISUAL: NTT Do Co Mo is the first mobile brand in the
world to seriously accomodate elderly users

In Europe, for some years a network of specialists have been working to improve the design of products for the over 50s. In liaison with the European Commission, they created the 'Design for Ageing Network' association which develops and tests products in hospitals and in people's homes before persuading companies to manufacture and market them.

We should mention also the setting up in September 2001 by two well-known designers of a very original international design agency, based in Paris and specialising in generational design. Called 'Age Design', its objective is to assist businesses that have understood that there is 'a life after 50'and that brands, products, packagings and architectures need to be adapted to win the interest and loyalty of those customers.

Finally, to conclude this topic, we would underline the relative aspect of anyone's judgement of their own health. What counts here is the person's morale. Two people suffering from the same illness can have diametrically opposed attitudes to it. One may dramatise the condition and be depressed and complain about it; another may take a positive view and be courageous and philosophical. Seeing the 'half-full glass' is a question of character.

A study published in November 1993, and carried out by Mintel using a sample of 5000 British people, shows that the older generations consider that their life continues to improve and have even a strong inclination to believe that their life is much better than when they were younger (Table 5.8). The same study had been carried out in 1988. There was a general improvement in the scores.

Table 5.8 Percentage of people more satisfied now than when they were younger

	1988	1992
Total over 50 years	33	38
Men	34	43
Women	31	34
50–54 years	46	47
55–59 years	40	47
60–64 years	29	39
65–69 years	23	38
70 years and over	24	28

Source: Mintel, UK

The French magazine for the over 50s, *Notre Temps*, invited its readers in 1996 to give their views on a large number of topics. More than 102,000 of them responded. This unprecedented poll produced a mine of information about the morale of the over 50s. The figures showed that 82% of people over 65 claimed to be quite or very happy and 77% considered themselves to be in good health.

The attitude towards the ageing of one's body is radically different from individual to individual, but also depends on the age one has reached.

The National Center for Health Statistics has studied the perception that people aged over 65 have about their own health. A large number, 70%, claim that their health is good or excellent compared with other people of the same age. Less than one-third judge it to be average or bad. 'Others are ill, not me!'

In 1988, in the UK, 40% of people aged over 65, when interviewed for the General Household Survey, described their health as 'good', 37% as 'fairly good' and 23% as 'not good'.

The lengthening of the lifespan is accompanied by a constant improvement in the health of old people. The decennial investigation into the health of the French made by INSEE in 1991 showed that nearly 80% of people aged 65 to 70 had no form of incapacity.

The Inserm researchers established that the average period when suffering severe or moderate incapacity (that is, confined to home, in a retirement home or hospice, even for three days or for an influenza attack) had decreased between 1981 and 1991.

In 1991, it was 9.1 for men and 12.6 years for women. In ten years, it had reduced by 6 months for men and one-tenth of a year for women. One of the two researchers, Pierre Mormiche, concludes his study with the words: 'It is certain that the years gained are entirely years of good health.'

Fourth preconception – they are resistant to novelty

Marketing managers think that the over 50s have acquired fixed consumption habits and there is no point in offering them new products. This false idea is based one undeniable truth: they remain faithful to a product that they are satisfied with. With age, after so much experience one favours brands that have proved satisfactory; this is only natural. Why change if one is satisfied? The TGI Gold study in 1998 in the UK showed that 55% of the over 50s rarely changed brands, but the same study also showed that 38% of them 'often try something new after seeing an ad', 59% are 'always prepared to try new products'.

We saw in Chapter 4 that the over 50s are far from resistant to new products and innovations. Why should they be? What principle should make one hostile to anything new after the age of 50?

A famous American investigation studied the relationship between the over 50s and new products. It was carried out by Goldring & Company and it analysed food consumption over 12 months.

From the set of markets involved, more than 75% of interviewees had tried a new product during the year:

- 45% had tested a new brand of cereal

- 34% a new brand of ice cream

- 30% a new brand of soup

- 30% a new brand of soft drink

- 22% a new brand of frozen fruit juice.

In July 1996, Senioragency carried out a study on French 50+ relating to different aspects of their consumption. One of the topics concerned the buying of new products. The results are instructive. To the question 'Do you buy new products?', 87% of the 50–59 group replied yes, as did 81% of 60–74 group and 76% of the over 75s.

Let us consider the market for video cameras. We imagine that they are bought by young couples who have just had children and want to record their children growing up. However, when one questions the chain retailers of electronic goods, one finds that the big buyers of such goods seem to be grandparents rather than parents. They want to be able to film scenery (because they travel a lot) as much as their family. The manufacturers of video cameras quickly detected the increased sales to the over 50s and radically simplified their new models. The Sharp brand was the first to take advantage of the vast potential of this market with its ViewCam model (see visual). Being extremely simple to operate, the ViewCam allows the user to hold the camera at arm's length, a feature of real progress for all over 50s who generally wear glasses. In Europe the advertising campaign featured a grandfather with his granddaughter.

Close to this market are video recorders, which also appeal to the over 50s. They allow them to view films, reports and programmes that they are fond of. But have you tried to program one of the latest generation machines? It is an almost impossible task (paradoxically, it has become easier to operate a computer than to master this widespread device). International statistics highlight the problem: 70% of people only use their

VISUAL: A manufacturer that has integrated ease of use into the design of its product. Result – a video camera that is ideal for the over 50s market

video recorder to play back cassettes, and only 7% know how to program a recording. One manufacturer's remote control device has no less than 64 buttons! What normal person can master such complexity, without electronic eyes and laser-guided fingers?

Driven furious by such complexity, two brilliant Chinese Americans came up with a marvellous device. Called Show View, it can control any video recorder by means of a simple code sent out by each TV transmission. As soon as this product was launched, it was enthusiastically received by American over 50s. Tens of millions of the devices were sold throughout the world within a few years.

Needless to say, this simplicity appealed to everyone. Show View is now included with all brands of video recorder. If a product works for the over 50s, it has a strong chance of being adopted by the younger generations.

The over 50s are therefore not hostile to novelty and even the most modern technologies. It is just that they have not grown up with a Gameboy, like our children.

How can we avoid saying something about the spectacular passion of the over 50s for multimedia computing and the Internet? They are greatly fascinated by this technology and for a number of good reasons. By switching on their PC, they are connecting with 'modernity' and thus remain in the know. CD-Roms and the Internet allow them to enjoy their favourite pursuits (history, genealogy, art, and so on), all from the comfort of their own home. Finally, not least of their motivations, by mastering these instruments of communication they are putting themselves on an equal footing with the younger generations and showing that they are not old and crabby. Multimedia creates a powerful inter-generation attraction, 'Come and see grandma and grandpa, I will show you my latest CD-Roms and some new Internet sites!' There, again, who has the time to surf the Internet, if not they? Microsoft and AARP (American Association of Retired Persons) got together to launch an enormous operation for the free training of American pensioners consisting of 500 seminars of Internet and multimedia training in the 30 largest cities. The aim was to train 50,000 people in the first phase of the operation; these people would then carry on the initiative themselves.

The Seniornet network that was launched in the USA some years ago was the first to appreciate the growing enthusiasm of the over 50s for the Internet. This has now been transformed into a giant portal called 'thirdage.com'.

Created in February, 1997 in its first form, Senior-Planet (http://www.seniorplanet.fr) is the first generalist French language site dedicated to the over 50s. It has proved very successful with French over 50s who are keen

VISUAL: RATP helps to remove the complexity of technology by introducing the over 50s to multimedia; a strategic way of getting close to the leisure expectations of this group of customers

VISUALS: Two of the leading portals dedicated to the over 50s –
www.thirdage.com and www.seniorplanet.fr

to make up for lost time. Senior surfers spend a lot more time on the Internet than other generations, they make more frequent visits and spend a lot of time sending e-mails, having the highest usage rate among private users. The growth rate of over 50s on the Web is on average twice that of those under 50 throughout the world. In the USA, some 25% of Internet users are over 50. The figure for Sweden is 22%, for the UK and Germany around 20%; for France, Italy and Spain, around 15–17%. 'Grey power' is gradually taking over the Net!

We should also congratulate RATP (the Parisian transport system: metro, bus and suburban trains), on their initiative in providing free computer training for the over 50s every Thursday at the Palais de la Découverte in Paris since January 1997. This was one of the schemes conceived by the organisation as part of its 'Over 50s Thursdays from the RATP'('les jeudis seniors de la RATP'), a promotion to suggest ideas of things for them to do. This helped to foster the goodwill of this section of their customers who are always on the lookout for new projects. Other Thursdays are devoted to gardening, cinema, dancing and genealogy.

CHAPTER 6

The USA – pioneers in marketing to the over 50s

You know you are old when the
candles cost more than the cake
BOB HOPE

An awareness of age

Every day, 6000 Americans enter their 50s. There are 75 million over 50s in the USA; in 2020 there will be 115 million. We should not forget that the baby boom, which lasted from 1946 to 1964, was especially large there, with 76 million births. The first baby boomers, born in 1946, are now aged 55. It is not surprising that the Americans, always quick to see a market, very soon understood the enormous potential of this population whose incomes greatly exceed the average US income. For a good 20 years, the marketing community have begun to attack the 50+ target by persuading, with some difficulty, businesses and advertisers. One should not imagine that from the outset everyone in the USA shared the conviction of the early pioneers of over 50s marketing. For a long time they were talking to deaf ears.

But opportunism and pragmatism are two well-known qualities of American managers. Faced with mounting facts and statistics, many businesses sought help from consultants in order to establish their strategy towards the Mature Market or the 50+ Consumers. 'Gray is gold' became a famous slogan in Madison Avenue, centre of the New York advertising world. Having inaugurated an advertising prize, the Age Wave company hands out awards regularly for the best campaigns and new products aimed specifically at the over 50s.

Several hundred companies, in all areas, have taken specific approaches over the past 15 years. From the numerous failures and errors, a set of lessons and rules have emerged, which are today of particular value for the American and international marketing community. From studying the attitudes and behaviour of the over 50s on an international scale, one can establish a great similarity of needs, expectations and behaviours from one country to the next (this was one of my biggest surprises when I began to work in the Japanese market). However, it should not be said that they are all identical; this would be quite wrong, given the diversity of segments at the heart of the over 50s population and the psychological differences between the American continent and old Europe. In short, it is striking to note that financial and material conditions, expectations with regard to products and services from companies, and attitudes to advertising campaigns, are very similar whatever the country involved.

This leads one to think that knowledge about the target 50+ market in the USA is, to a large extent, exploitable and exportable to Europe. Here the term 'exportable' is, in this case, particularly heavy in meaning for Europe-based businesses. One therefore asks oneself the question: When are the large American corporations going to perceive the huge potential of the 120 million over 50s in Europe, with a purchasing power greater than that of their contemporaries in the USA (thanks to the excellence of the social security systems in Europe)?

Speaking of marketing to the over 50s in the USA leads us on to examine the working of AARP, which has acted on their behalf, and continues to preserves the privileges of greying America.

American Association of Retired Persons – the world's strongest lobby

Creation of the AARP

In 1947, Ethel Andrus, a former headteacher, created the NRTA (National Retired Teachers Association) which brought together a number of retired teachers. The aim of NRTA at the time was to help with its members' retirement and tax problems.

In 1958, Ethel Andrus realised that the problems faced by retired American teachers were shared by all those over 50.

At the time, there was no health insurance for private individuals (the Medicare Health Care Act dates from 1965), and insurance companies refused to provide health cover for those over 50. After several attempts, Ethel Andrus finally found an insurer to cover the NRTA members for a trial period. This proved successful, and the insurance company agreed to provide cover for NRTA members.

From then on, many people, retired or not, wanted to join NFTA in order to be able to obtain health cover. Ethel Andrus then decided to create an organisation open to all those over 50, whether working or retired. This was AARP. In 1982, NRTA was absorbed by AARP and became a special subdivision.

Subsequently, AARP developed its own pharmacy mail-order service to satisfy its members' requirements for medication. Today, this service is the world's largest mail-order supplier of medicines. The AARP Pharmacy Catalogue contains more than 1200 medicines and health aids, and more than 30 million copies are sent out every quarter.

The basic principles of AARP are:

■ To promote the independence and dignity of old people

■ To improve the life of American over 50s by offering them services defending their rights and informing them about them

■ To encourage the over 50s 'to serve, not to be served'.

Long-term objectives:

■ To provide quality services for members

■ To campaign for all to be able to have access to health security

■ To underline the dignity and equality of all at their place of work

■ To reduce poverty

■ To carry out research to better understand and identify the needs of the older population.

The expansion of AARP and the reasons for its success

In 1958, AARP had 50,000 members. Today, there are more than 32 million, that is, 12% of the total American population, amounting to nearly one out of every two Americans over 50.

**OUR MEMBERS ARE 50.
IT'S THE SPEED LIMIT THAT'S 65.**

AARP members are definitely not riding off into the sunset. They're fit, fun and ready for more. Why not join them? For just $10 you and your spouse can get information on everything from finance to fitness. You'll have access to prescription savings and quality insurance programs. AARP can be your advocate in Washington and help you get involved in local AARP projects. There's also a great magazine, the *AARP Bulletin* and lots of discounts. Find out for yourself. To join, simply complete and mail the coupon below, with your payment today!

AARP

www.aarp.org

Join AARP Today.

Membership includes a magazine subscription and the *AARP Bulletin*. Plus dozens of free publications, seminars and volunteer opportunities. You don't even have to be retired to join. Just 50 or older. So send for your Membership Kit today.

Dues are not deductible for income tax purposes. One membership includes spouse. Annual dues include $2.40 for a magazine subscription and $.85 for *AARP Bulletin*. Dues outside U.S. domestic mail limits $10/one year. Please allow six weeks for delivery of Membership Kit.

☐ One year/$10   ☐ Three years/$27 (Save 10%)

Your Name (please print)_____

Address_____ Apt._____

City_____ State_____ Zip_____

Date of Birth _____ / _____ / _____
                Month   Day   Year

☐ I work full time. ☐ I work part time. ☐ I'm retired. H2RAK

Spouse's Name (please print)_____

Date of Birth _____ / _____ / _____
                Month   Day   Year

☐ Check or money order enclosed, payable to AARP. (Send no cash, please.)

☐ Please bill me later.

☐ If you're an active or retired educator, check here to join the NRTA Division of AARP.   H2RNK

Mail coupon to:
**AARP Membership Center
PO Box 199
Long Beach, CA 90801**

VISUAL: Harley Davidson — yes, the new over 50s like to enjoy themselves and AARP is well aware of it!

In parallel with this exponential growth in membership, AARP broadened its activities by creating new programmes and services (such as a training programme to assist women in managing their accounts, since this work was done generally by a deceased husband). To make membership 'essential', AARP had the idea of negotiating with a large number of players in the fields of industry, tourism and services, special offers and significant discounts for those with a membership card. Some examples are: General Motors, Best Western, Avis, Marriott, Gateway, Sun Holidays. Since 2001, AARP has introduced a label which identifies its partners as 'AARP approved'. Its turnover now exceeds $550 million. To allow its members to get in touch very quickly, it has established its own Internet site at www.aarp.org.

With such backing, *Fortune* magazine consistently places AARP at the top of the most powerful American lobbies, well ahead of the famous National Rifle Association that defends the right to bear arms and which 'only' has 2.5 million members.

Effective decentralisation

AARP has created 4000 local AARP offices and 2500 associations of retired teachers. The latter provide valuable local support and allow members to meet one another. Supported by the 1700 permanent staff, more than 400,000 voluntary pensioners participate in the multiple activities of the association.

Every day, many new applications for membership arrive at the association's head office in Washington DC. The reasons for the attraction stem from the fact that to become a member of AARP does not cost much ($10 for a year or $27 for three years). This entitles members to receive the magazine *Modern Maturity* (for the retired and, from Spring 2001, the magazine *My Generation* for those baby boomers still working), six times a year, and the *AARP Bulletin* 11 times a year (see visual) .

To illustrate the strength of the relationship between AARP and American over 50s, the association receives some 7000 letters per day.

Surpassing the famous *Reader's Digest*, *TV Guide*, and the other US 50+ magazines, such as *New Choices*, *Mature Outlook* or *Lear's*, the magazines *Modern Maturity* and *My Generation* have the largest print-runs with 21.3 million copies. *Modern Maturity* has many local editions and began to accept advertisements from 1980. These are subjected to close scrutiny from the publishers and their advertising department. Would-be advertisers must demonstrate that their product is really suited

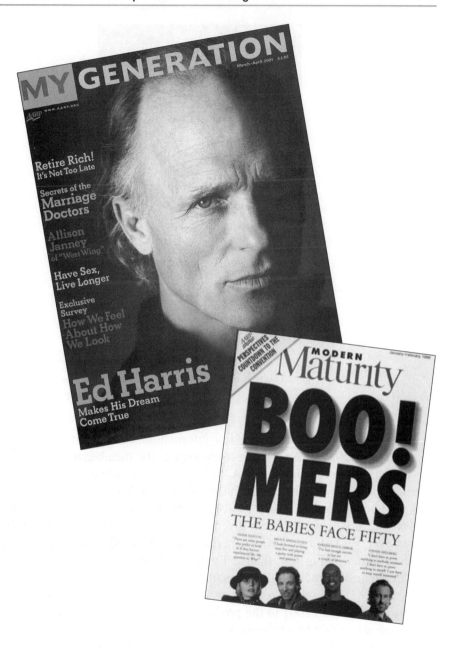

VISUAL: *Modern Maturity*, the version for pensioners; *My Generation*, launched in Spring 2001, aimed at baby boomers. *Modern Maturity* and *My Generation*, the largest print-runs of the US magazine press

VISUAL: AARP. Life before 50 is nothing but
a warm up – a very apt slogan

to the needs of the over 50s. For information, the cost of a four-colour
page is $250,000! As for direct marketing, the membership list is never
leased out; it remains under AARP's control to ensure that any product
promoted is well suited to the needs of the over 50s.

Although to date AARP has been content to transmit TV programmes
via existing networks, it has given much thought to buying and launching
an over 50s radio station in America which it would control. It is considered that, costing less than a TV network, it would serve as an ideal
complement to their publications.

After 25 years of experience, the publishers of *Modern Maturity*
moved in March 2001 to the production of two editions of the magazine.
There are in fact two types of reader, over 50s who are still working and
an older group of pensioners who obviously do not have quite the same
needs and attitudes. 'Our aim would be to have as many different versions
as there are types of reader', the chief editor stated when explaining the
aims of the appeal to the new generations of over 50s coming from the
baby boom.

AARP — powerful lobby

One of the aims of AARP is to educate and inform opinion leaders and the public about the realities and challenges that await an America whose population includes a considerable mass of people over 50.

Despite the diversity of its membership, AARP has undertaken to defend the rights of all. This is why so many people enrol. The association's mission is to represent American over 50s in matters of legislation and regulation, both at the federal and at state level. In parallel, it also encourages them to take an interest in political, legislative and judicial problems in the USA.

By means of the publication *Summary of AARP Federal Public Policy*, AARP informs legislators and administrators of inequalities in the law and lobbies for them to revise defective laws.

There are three special units that aid AARP in this mission:

- The AARP Public Policy Institute, established in 1985, it conducts all research into problems linked with age and analyses state politics that concern them

- The Survey Design and Analysis Department undertakes to question the American people (members and non-members) on a number of topics

- The Forecasting and Environmental Scanning Department evaluates the future changes in American society, concentrating on technology, demography, education, health insurance, family structure, relationships between generations and the ecological environment.

The *AARP Bulletin* is used to inform all its members about legislation and programmes that concern the over 50s. Articles analyse the forthcoming actions and alterations to government policy and lobby members to convey their opinion to their representatives.

For its part, AARP sees to it that the legislators are permanently informed as to its views on such and such a law. It has the power to form a coalition with other national associations and support or reject a given law.

AARP/Vote is the programme for the education of electors. Its aim is to make electors and candidates aware of the problems of elderlyAmericans.

All of these activities have contributed to make AARP the powerful mouthpiece for Americans over 50s. It is therefore an unavoidable organisation in the USA, envied both at home and abroad. It has at it disposition some 20 full-time lobbyists to defend its position in Congress and the Senate.

This said, despite its power and its considerable membership, AARP has for several years complained of its difficulty in recruiting new members. Membership figures appear to have 'stagnated' at around the 32 million mark. The baby-boom generations apparently are less willing to be members of an association for the defence of pensioners. AARP has undertaken an extensive programme of strategic repositioning; for example, the initials are no longer spelled out in full (the word 'retired' does not ring well). The launch of *My Generation* in March 2001 was an important deliberate act. The magazine's title is especially pertinent to have a chance of appealing to the generation that has always cultivated its difference and given pride of place to enjoyment, thus earning the writer, Tom Wolfe's, name the 'Me generation'.

To underline the correctness of AARP's change of direction, we would mention a study carried out by Rupert Starck who asked over 50s which song described their feelings and expectations about their retirement. Almost half of the over 55s chose 'Born to be Wild', while those over 65 wanted a bit more peace and quiet, since 68% of them chose 'The Sound of Silence'.

Modern Maturity's role in promoting marketing to 50+

Since its launch *Modern Maturity* has had the role of educator and trainer, to make the American marketing community aware of the over 50s as a target market, and to show the level of tact required in addressing this section of the market. This communication strategy is based on a very simple idea: in order to attract and retain advertisers, the management of the magazine help them to develop advertising campaigns that will generate the highest possible response. In fact, the magazine staff know better than anyone the expectations and tastes of their 30 million or so readers, which is a fair enough sample of the over 50s population of the USA.

In order to reach advertisers and agencies, the magazine has for a long time taken double pages of advertising in the two national trade journals, *Advertising Age* and *Adweek*. These advertisements demonstrate the importance of the over 50s in markets as diverse as cars, cereals, dairy products and chocolate bars. They are aimed at dispelling the preconceptions of advertisers and agencies that only the young are volume consumers.

But the true innovation of *Modern Maturity* was when 15 years ago it published widely a series of very didactic advertisements called '*Modern Maturity* advertising lessons'. Classics of their kind, these advertisements consist of pieces of advice and insights into the attitudes of the over 50s, all of great value to campaign designers for that market.

CHAPTER 7

The wrong approach – how to alienate the over 50s

*If you are fifty or over, even if you feel quite fit, read to
live another fifty years, be aware that for advertising
people you do not count; for them, you are
already dead and, if you are dead for the
advertisers and promoters, you do not
count for much for the TV channels*
BERNARD PIVOT, FAMOUS FRENCH COLUMNIST

It can turn out that promotion and marketing managers behave like real
sorcerer's apprentices when they commit what one might call the crime of
'brand suicide', whether voluntarily or involuntarily. Every year, the International Cannes Advertising Film Festival, shows an anthology of TV
spots from around the world that present 'old' people in a ridiculous and
distasteful way in order to show other younger consumer generations that
such and such a brand dismisses elderly consumers out of hand. For a
creative director, mocking the elderly in an ad increases the chances of
taking home a prize, since the jury, consisting of other creative people,
regularly votes for films in which the joke is on the elderly. Since the over
50s are considered as nothing in the business, why not enjoy making fun
of them?

The aim of this chapter is to identify the errors that have damaged the
image of some brands in the eyes of millions of 50+ consumers – errors
that could often have been avoided. Some are even clear provocations that
would drive over 50s to boycott the brand. Brand owners should be aware

that, given the significant increase in life expectancy, alienating someone of this age group runs the risk of losing a customer for 25–30 years. An instructive point, perhaps?

Confining them to the ghetto of age and its problems

No one over 50 wants to have their age pointed out to them. It is humiliating and discriminatory. Growing old is already a test; there is no need to make it the basis of an argument or an advertisement. Three famous cases come to mind: Gerber, Affinity and Attends. They have been quoted regularly by US experts in generational marketing, such as Ken Dychtwald, Kurt Medina, Jeff Ostroff, David Wolfe and Carol Morgan.

The Gerber brand of baby foods in small jars had established that in the USA many old people were buying their products, not for their grandchildren, but for themselves. They were interested in the products because they had dental problems, delicate stomachs or needed a diet with balanced vitamin content.

Gerber thought that it had found a very good marketing opportunity and decided to launch a range of dishes called Senior Citizen. It was received as an insult. The product caused an outcry and was rapidly removed from the shelves.

Until then, buyers had been able to go through the cash desk with others thinking that the baby foods were for their grandchildren. But now, the advertising made it clear to every shopper that they were for the elderly. This they could not bear.

The giant cosmetics corporation Johnson & Johnson had a similar misadventure with its shampoo brand Affinity, which had been created for the hair of women aged over 45. In all innocence, the packaging and the advertising campaign underlined this specific age group with no tact. The result was catastrophic and the brand was made aware that no woman likes to be reminded that her hair grows old. Once rid of all mention of age, the product was repositioned in the market and developed normally.

The situation with Attends is similar. Procter & Gamble, whose marketing competence cannot be contested, is in the incontinence products market with its Attends range. The advertising launch in the USA was based on a very clinical description (with numerous abdominal diagrams) of the reasons why some people become incontinent. As though the victims of incontinence did not already know! They were seeking a solution to their problem, not a call to order! As might be expected, Attends did not meet their needs with this first advertising campaign.

Using a label to identify a product or service aimed at the over 50s is a sensitive issue. The most common approach is to use a description such as 'over 50s', '50 years and over', 'Senior' or 'golden age'. The rule is to test thoroughly in advance the reaction of the target market to the labelling of the product or service in question. This works very well in the case of specific insurance ('Zuritel, the No. 1 specialist car insurer for pensioners', launched successfully in France by the Zurich Group) or the different products and services for the over 50s promoted by Saga, the large specialist for British pensioners, or the subscription that offers special deals to the over 50s (Avis Club Senior), or some special event for them (the RATP Over 50s Thursdays). Another example is an Internet portal which clearly states its target audience in a medium where the vast majority of the brands on the Web have no precise meaning (for example www.seniorplanet.fr, or www.seniornett. no, or www.senior.com).

But this will probably not apply when one considers mass consumption products, such as foods, where over-precise labelling runs the risk of alienating buyers. In such cases, one must resort to circumlocution and specific advertising campaigns broadcast via targeted media (day-time TV and the over 50s press).

VISUAL: K par K – does this brand seriously believe that consumers will be attracted by this lady?

Showing them as soured, spiteful, ridiculous or physically dependent

Taking the easy way out, many promoters responsible for a mass market product or one aimed at a young market use the over 50s as a foil. Their campaigns are offensive to the over 50s. They give a degrading image to this age group and do not achieve the desired effect; they do not appeal to the young or the old. For example, the poster campaign by Axion Banking in Belgium, had heavy impact but small success in the end. At an International Cannes Advertising Film Festival, where the advertising profession rewards campaigns that use the over 50s as victims, an Argentinian

VISUAL: Yamaha could have enhanced the qualities of this product for 50+; they preferred to choose this old lady!

campaign for Cindor-Shake showed an adolescent using the trembling hand of his Parkinson's disease suffering grandfather to shake his tin of fruit juice. Or again, the British Harley-Davidson campaign that featured a old man with a Zimmer frame who complains that his son, who had promised to buy him an electric mobile chair, bought a motor cycle instead. The final slogan is revealing: 'Harley-Davidson: the most irresponsible thing to do!' But in fact, what business can afford to deprive itself of such a large and influential market?

In the Netherlands, Yamaha ran a targeted press campaign (*Plus* magazine) for their electric cycles, ideally suited to the needs of the over 50s, that featured exaggerated and ridiculous pictures of older women (see visual). What advertiser could believe that someone over 50 would want to identify with such caricatures? One of the key functions of advertising is to enable the consumers to recognise themselves and imagine themselves using the product on offer. As soon as the over 50s are involved, the advertisers appear to forget this basic principle.

VISUAL: Axion banking wants it to be clear: 'we don't want seniors in our bank'! (Belgium)

Portraying them crudely

Levi's, the jeans and sportswear manufacturers, who were anxious to reclaim some of the young customers that they had been losing to other, new and more trendy brands, were unable to come up with anything better in the UK than depicting an old couple sprawling on a bench in bathing suits and with the slogan: 'Age doesn't improve everything'. English humour, perhaps, but over the top. Nudity is not something that generally appeals to the over 50s. Throughout the world, the generations in this age group are quite modest and prudish. No one likes the idea of becoming old and this campaign portrayed the ravages of time too crudely. The over 50s like to identify themselves with people who grow old in dignity and honesty; it is not appropriate to remind them of the outward signs of age. Even if Levi's advertising is not designed to appeal to the over 50s, why does this brand try to cut itself off from this fringe of consumers, unless they have never seen people of that age group in jeans? Have they forgotten that many over 50s have always known and used the brand

VISUAL: Levi's seem to forget that 50+ grew up with their brand

because of its quality and robustness? It seems that the boundary between 'ageism' and 'racism' is very narrow.

We cannot also fail to mention a campaign that caused a scandal in Switzerland. This was launched by the third largest Swiss health insurer SWICA and involved a single tariff policy, irrespective of age or sex. The TV and cinema spot shows a 70-year-old couple making love in the nude in front of the camera (with no anatomical details missing) and with the catch-line 'for him, she will be always 30 ...'. Of course, the film was acclaimed by the advertising profession for its impertinence and creativity, but it profoundly shocked the overwhelming majority of the Swiss over 50s who are not renowned for their progressive and tolerant attitude. The agency responsible for the campaign achieved some notoriety in the Swiss market, but the result for the advertiser as far as the senior generations were concerned was disastrous. But then, does that matter, since they only amount to a third of the Swiss population?

Presenting them as what they are not

All products being mixed together, advertising agencies also have a tendency to overdo things. It is easy to denigrate the effects of age. That is why some advertising managers judge it opportune to take the other point of view and portray the over 50s either as 'supermen' or as 'superbrains'. Although this idealisation may be less degrading, it is no more appropriate, and it is doubtful if it will appear credible to the 50+. At all events, it indicates a misunderstanding of the target market by the agencies and their advertisers. The over 50s are not dupes. They know perfectly well what they are capable of physically. Portraying them as supermen is not going to make them consider the product. Remember that the over 50s are rational and appreciate especially offers that are well supported and argued (they are great readers of catalogues and brochures). This type of communication runs the risk of arousing their mistrust and suspicion. Nevertheless, they appreciate wit and are aware that artistic licence allows the distortion of characters and situations. They can therefore decode what is entertaining and what is not.

An example is the campaign run in France by Volkswagen for the launch of their people carrier, the Sharan. In a very lively film two 80-year-olds remember the time when they bought their Sharan and sing while moving about to a current rap song. The film was a great success with the young families that the vehicle was designed for. It pleased some over 50s and displeased others who did not like to see old people acting like children. But what disgusted the majority of the over 50s was the accompanying 4m × 3m poster showing an old couple kissing full on the mouth (see visual). At that age, one is still in love, but some modesty and delicacy is appreciated. This ostentatious embrace rang false and shocked the 50+, even the most modernistic of them.

VISUAL: Volkswagen — this ostentatious embrace
shocked the over 50s (France)

CHAPTER 8

The keys to success – how to win over the over 50s

The 50+ are not hard of hearing ... the problem is that
businesses don't speak the right language
JEAN MARC SEGATI, SENIORAGENCY INTERNATIONAL

We have already seen the considerable importance of the over 50s for the economy and for the different consumer markets. But if one compares the consumption of a pensioner household with that of a working family household, one sees a slight deficit of 5% between the two. If the 50+ were to allocate to consumption the same proportion of their resources as the other categories of the population, the result would be billions of euros or dollars of additional spending.

The challenge of this chapter is to show what methods and techniques have to be employed in order to appeal to the over 50s with the language, products and services that they truly expect.

Marketing specific needs and standard needs

Faced with the growing importance of the over 50s, every business has to ask itself the question: how do we get to understand this market?

One of the most effective options is to create and develop specific products, services and communications. Another is simply to take the over 50s into account in the marketing and promotional planning, while still continuing to exploit products and services destined for a much wider public.

Marketing specific needs

Specialised products and services provide a solution to the effects of age. Ageing leads to physical and social consequences, and means that high technology products become more difficult to deal with. We shall analyse some examples of the marketing opportunities that this can create. Tables 8.1, 8.2 and 8.3 give examples of products and services targeted at particular types of need.

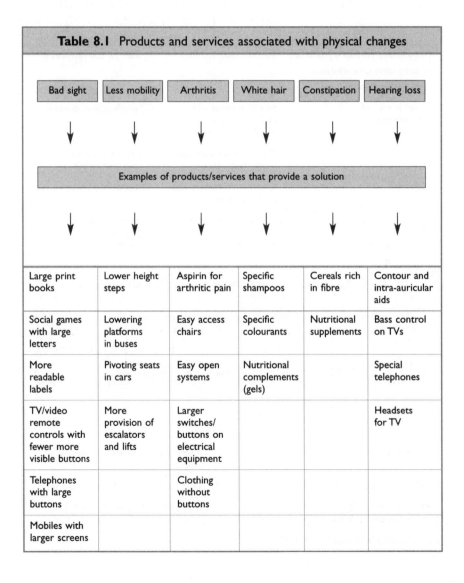

Table 8.1 Products and services associated with physical changes

Bad sight	Less mobility	Arthritis	White hair	Constipation	Hearing loss

Examples of products/services that provide a solution

Bad sight	Less mobility	Arthritis	White hair	Constipation	Hearing loss
Large print books	Lower height steps	Aspirin for arthritic pain	Specific shampoos	Cereals rich in fibre	Contour and intra-auricular aids
Social games with large letters	Lowering platforms in buses	Easy access chairs	Specific colourants	Nutritional supplements	Bass control on TVs
More readable labels	Pivoting seats in cars	Easy open systems	Nutritional complements (gels)		Special telephones
TV/video remote controls with fewer more visible buttons	More provision of escalators and lifts	Larger switches/ buttons on electrical equipment			Headsets for TV
Telephones with large buttons		Clothing without buttons			
Mobiles with larger screens					

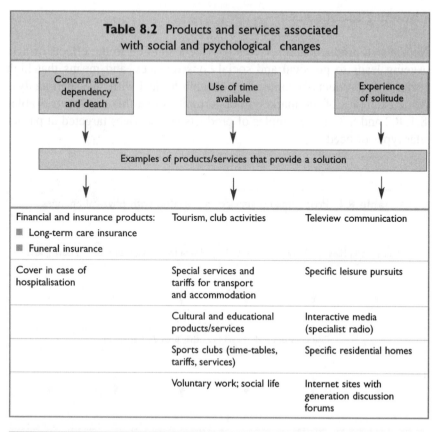

Table 8.2 Products and services associated with social and psychological changes

Concern about dependency and death	Use of time available	Experience of solitude
Examples of products/services that provide a solution		
Financial and insurance products: ■ Long-term care insurance ■ Funeral insurance	Tourism, club activities	Teleview communication
Cover in case of hospitalisation	Special services and tariffs for transport and accommodation	Specific leisure pursuits
	Cultural and educational products/services	Interactive media (specialist radio)
	Sports clubs (time-tables, tariffs, services)	Specific residential homes
	Voluntary work; social life	Internet sites with generation discussion forums

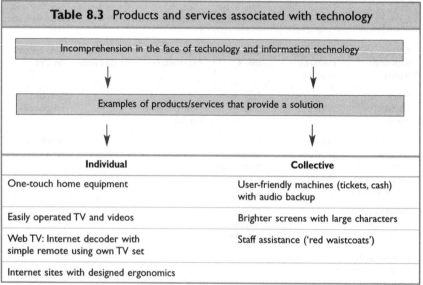

Table 8.3 Products and services associated with technology

Incomprehension in the face of technology and information technology

Examples of products/services that provide a solution

Individual	Collective
One-touch home equipment	User-friendly machines (tickets, cash) with audio backup
Easily operated TV and videos	Brighter screens with large characters
Web TV: Internet decoder with simple remote using own TV set	Staff assistance ('red waistcoats')
Internet sites with designed ergonomics	

Success stories

In the USA, Europe, Japan and elsewhere, businesses have produced specific products and services that meet the expectations of the over 50s. We shall give some examples.

Foods and nutritional complements:

- Wrigley's has created a Freedent range of chewing gum suitable for dentures

- Mineral water producer Talians, belonging to the Danone group, targets the over 50s. It is rich in calcium (to combat osteoporosis) and has a large, easily opened cap specially designed for arthritic hands

- Quaker Oats and Kellogg's have developed products that are rich in fibre to combat constipation problems

- The dairy industry has appreciated the great potential of this market, with products such as 'Ram Calcio' in Spain, 'Nestlé Omega Plus' in Brazil and 'Candia Calcium Plus' in France

- More and more nutritional complements are positioned for the over 50s. In the USA and Canada: 'Boost', 'Resource' and 'Ensure'; 'Vitaviva' in Italy

- 'Longlife' drinks are becoming a big market around the world (a four-fold increase in sales since 1998 in the USA). Brands include 'Tree Life Diet Balanced Drink', 'Alvita Long Life' (green tea) and in Japan the 'Refresh Eye' drink.

Books:

- Series of books printed in large typefaces have appeared: 16 Body, Doubleday, and the 'Lecture confort' series from France Loisirs.

Household equipment:

- The 'Softouch' scissors produced by the Fiskars brand, designed to be easy for the over 50s to use. They were a huge success; sales were ten times higher than expected

- The Oxo brand of kitchen utensils, 'Good Grip', developed for those suffering from arthritis. Extensive marketing intelligence produced a design that is functional, modern and trendy.

Accommodation:

■ The range of 'Maisons Seniors' designed by the Architects group in France.

Mail-order sales:

■ Catalogues from firms, such as Daxon, Bleu-Bonheur, Afibel, Anne Weyburn and Damart, have been able to secure market share among over 50s women through the size ranges, designs and colours offered.

Public transport:

■ The lowering platform buses introduced by RATP in France in January 1996 and the 'easy read' Metro map (especially readable) introduced in February 1998

■ 'Senior Pass' card passes introduced by the railways in many countries.

Bicycles:

■ The City 800 and 805 Special Senior bicycles marketed by Peugeot and the Yamaha electric cycles called PAS.

VISUAL: L'Oréal is aware that mature women are the
prime target for hair coloration products

Cosmetics:

- The Nivea Vital range focused the attention of competing brands on the market potential of the over 50s. Competing products quickly appeared: Resilience Lift from Estée Lauder, Age Perfect from L'Oréal, Novadiol from Vichy, Elsève's Regenium, and so on.

Insurance and finance:

- In France, Zuritel launched the first direct car insurance scheme for the over 60s in 1996 (see visual)

- Norwich Union, specialist in providing for the over 50s, with its funeral policy, available throughout Europe

- Saga insurance and financial services in the UK

- Direct Line car insurance in the UK

VISUAL: Zuritel had the brilliant idea of choosing the famous navigator Eric Tabarly to help it emerge rapidly into a very competitive market

- Axa Belgium with 'Happy Life'

- CGU Belgium with 'Forever Young'

- 'Golden Years' from the Bank of Ireland since 1980

- Cassa di Risparmio di Firenze in Italy with the 'Età libera' account and card

- The 'Super 55' account from the Caja Laboral Euskadiko Kutxa in Portugal

- 'Autonomie' insurance from Axa, France.

All the large insurance groups have launched, or are in the process of launching, funeral policies and long-term care insurance policies for elderly people.

VISUAL: Avis (in France) is the first car rental company to have designed a full package for 55+ customers

Cars:

- Avis launched their Club Senior in 1997 (a very successful French initiative – see visual)

- The dashboard of Saab's 900 series cars contains a screen that gives a simplified display of information that is updated at great speed. It takes account of people with slower reactions

- Since 1996, Renault has regarded the over 50s as a pilot market for their new models. Timed lighting on all doors to facilitate entry and exit is an example of the refinements that have emerged

- For its part, Ford is aware of the need to tailor the ergonomics and comfort of their vehicles to the needs of the older sector of their market. Hence the use of the 'third age suit' by their young designers and engineers to better understand the needs of older customers.

Retirement homes:

- The promoter Del Webb was the first to identify the needs of American pensioners as far as housing is concerned. In 1960, he built Sun City in the north of Phoenix, the first town intended for the over 55s. There are now more than ten such towns throughout the USA.

Furniture:

- Premier, a manufacturer of bathroom suites and showers, offers a range of walk-in 'Easy' baths (see visual)

- The Scandinavian 'Stressless' range of reclining chairs has long met the comfort needs of the over 50s and now enjoys Europe-wide success.

Telecommunications:

- AT&T in the USA and France Telecom offer a full range of products: large-button telephones, amplifiers, automatic emergency dialling

- In Japan, Sony and Sanyo offer large-button telephones that also allow the voice delivery speed of the caller to be slowed to make it more audible

- NTT Do Co Mo easy to use and read mobile phone in Japan.

'Brown' and 'white' goods:

- Whirlpool washing machines with large buttons

VISUAL: Premier Easy Bath – thanks to this, senior citizens
can continue to enjoy the pleasure of bathing

- The Show View simple programmer for video recorders
- The Panasonic Dimension 4 microwave oven with pre-programmed buttons
- The Thomson TV set remote control with only five buttons.

Media:

- The specialist magazines *Notre Temps* and *Pleine Vie* in France; *Saga Magazine, Yours* and *Choice* in the UK; *Plus* in Belgium and Holland; *Modern Maturity, My Generation, Mature Outlook, New Choices* and *Lear's* in the USA; *Good Times* and *Bel Age* in Canada; *Vi over 60* in Norway, and so on

- Large Internet portals aimed at 'modern 50+' keen to show that they are up-to-date and able to master the most symbolic icon of modernity and 'eternal youth'. We can mention: www.thirdage.com in the USA; www.vavo.com in the UK; www.seniorplanet.fr in France and www.seniorplanet.be in Belgium

- The French radio group NRJ focused its Nostalgie station on the baby boomers and young over 50s in contrast to all the other music station obsessed by the young audience. It has progressed to reach the position of second most popular music station in a very short time, owing to its very original marketing approach.

Tourism, accommodation services and transport:

There are no surprises here. For a long time specialist organisations have recognised the enormous potential of the over 50s, in particular, Saga in the UK. There are nowadays countless special offers and discounts to attract the over 50s during off-peak and low-volume periods.

In France, Selectour was the first to offer a specific catalogue for tourism (see visual).

We can also mention the shrewd approach of the American cruise company, Red Cruise Line, whose clientele contains a high proportion of women (many widows). To make its cruises more attractive, it created its Host Program. We should recall that the over 50s account for more than 70% of cruise customers (see, for example, Notre Temps, Pleine Vie or Saga senior cruises).

VISUAL: Over 50s represent 30% of the European tourist market; some specific brochures are now available

The Host Program offers very attractive rates to men over 50 who go on their cruises in the expectation that they will dine, dance and converse with single women. This initiative enabled the company to improve the men/women ratio, enliven the ambience and foster loyalty for future cruises. In short, a very successful piece of marketing.

The international hotel chains are also very interested in these potential customers who can help to fill the empty slots in their bookings during the non-business periods of the week or the low seasons. For example, the Scandinavian RICA hotels have introduced a Senior Pass, which allows one free night for every five nights booked, lower tariffs and specific tariffs for grandchildren. In 2001 the Mercure chain, belonging to the Accor group, introduced a special rate for couples over 55 at a much-reduced tariff: 'Two for the price of one' (see visual). For a long time, the American Best Western chain has targeted this age group in its marketing (see visual).

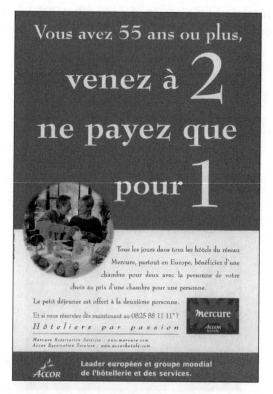

VISUAL: Accor is the first large European group to clearly focus one of its hotel chains towards mature clients

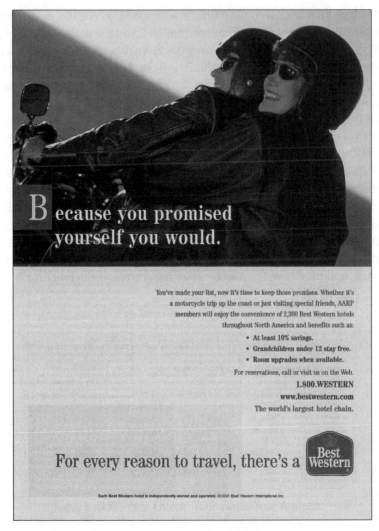

VISUAL: Best Western has very efficiently developed an
international 50+ marketing strategy to attract mature customers

Marketing of standard needs

First statement — little hope from the young

Some businesses consider that it would be too disturbing and, no doubt,
risky to make a specific appeal to the over 50s. There is always the fear of
tarnishing their image with age.

This legitimate concern ought to be alleviated, given the demographic facts and the economic difficulties that the youngest age groups face. Between 1984 and 1994, in several developed economies, there was a striking regression (worrying for the future) in the standard of living of the young generations, as shown in the different calculations carried out by Insee in France (see Table 8.4).

Is it therefore relevant to continue to concentrate 100% of marketing and promotion effort on the youngest age classes when they are motivated by what is cheapest? For certain products and services, this means that one has decided to ignore more than half of the potential customers. It is the younger generations that have enabled the hard-discount chains to develop in Europe, but these stores (Aldi, Lidl, Norma, Ed) are the denial of the brands. In comparison, it is known that less than 4% of the over 50s buy from such outlets. It cannot be emphasised enough that the 50+ are the true followers of brands; they recognise their quality and value, they are prepared to pay the price, and they have the means. They are the real 'brand victims'!

Table 8.4 Welfare index according to age: change from 1984–94

Age	Average standard of living *m* (in relative terms)			Gini G index intra age			Welfare *m* × (*I* − *G*) (in relative terms)		
	1984	1994	Change 1984–94	1984	1994	Change 1984–94	1984	1994	Change 1984–94
Under 30	92	75	−17	0.275	0.314	+0.039	100	80	−20
30–39	97	91	−6	0.299	0.316	+0.017	101	96	−5
40–49	99	98	−1	0.319	0.340	+0.021	101	100	−1
50–59	109	120	+11	0.359	0.410	+0.051	105	110	+5
60–69	106	110	+4	0.355	0.363	+0.008	103	109	+6
70–79	98	107	+9	0.375	0.353	−0.022	91	108	+17
80 and over	93	96	+3	0.368	0.373	+0.005	88	94	+6
Total	100	100	/	0.331	0.357	+0.026	100	100	/

Standard of living calculated with the Oxford consumption units and corrected inheritance income. How to read: the social welfare index is the synthesis between the average and the dispersion of the standards of living of each age band. The dispersion is evaluated by the Gini index. In 1994, the age band of the under 30s cumulates a relative lowering of the standard of living and a progression of disparities. The social welfare indicator of this age class is at its lowest (−20) indicating a particular degradation in the situation of these young households.
Source: Family Budget Investigation, Insee, France

Second statement — an under-utilised potential

The 50+ market is an important market. However, marketing managers do not make the effort to identify the specific needs and expectations of the over 50s. The result is a commercial loss that can be considerable. We should remember the sales maxim developed by IBM for its sales teams: 'To sell well, one must first shut one's mouth.' Keep quiet in order to listen to the client's expectations of a product or service. The first essential is to understand the client's needs, demands and requirements. This is the aim of this book: to help businesses make themselves aware that they have within reach consumers who ask no more than to be convinced, and that all they need to do is to make the effort to understand their specific needs and they will gain invaluable marketing information. By nature, the over 50s are not fickle. If they find a company that knows how to provide them with the products or services that they want, there is every chance that they will remain faithful customers for most of their life. The over 50s therefore need to be integrated with the other generations by making adaptations or corrections designed to satisfy them. In short, by making the offer conform to the expectation.

Third statement — the baby boomers arrive

Since 1 January, 1996, the baby boomers have come to swell the ranks of the over 50s. Being dominant in the cultural and economic fields, these millions of individuals have always taken an active attitude to consumption. This behaviour is not going to disappear when they turn 50.

They will continue to live in the same way and fundamentally transform the former image of the over 50s. Businesses must prepare themselves, from now, to communicate with this new consumer who, while close to younger target markets, will nevertheless have needs and constraints appropriate to his or her age.

All of these reasons drive the marketing and advertising managers to pay attention to the 50+. Those businesses that have understood soon enough will benefit before the others. Those businesses active on the American market have long acquired knowledge of how to market to the over 50s. It is a safe bet that they will not delay long before attacking the old continent and other parts of the world where the populations are ageing.

From offer to success – the required routes

Whether you have chosen the generational marketing or the transgenerational marketing approach, it is essential to follow certain required routes which are themselves a means of maintaining a commercial relationship with the over 50s.

Offer them benefits and price reductions

The first special tariffs and discount cards for the 'third age' (railway travel cards) appeared long ago. Old people had low incomes and it was necessary to 'subsidise' them by these specific discounts. It is a known fact that, currently, the reality is quite different for a large proportion of Masters, Liberated and even Peaceful.

But the custom is established. There is no longer any question of withdrawing this benefit that they cling to.

Offering them a special '50+' discount is clearly a good way of attracting them to a product or service. It is also a good way of getting them to try something, and to point them towards certain products, timetables and periods. Since 1997 American Express USA has operated its 'Senior membership program' for its pre-retirement members. This new scheme is offered with a reduced annual subscription for people over 62 and includes access to a whole range of benefits and reduced tariffs with Hertz, Continental Airlines, Marriott and Disney World. The message is clear: you are retired, you have money but we know that this is no reason to waste the hard-earned cash you have saved while working.

At the same time, one should recognise the limitations of this approach which, if used on its own, is relatively dangerous. It is an established fact that the over 50s most attracted by these offers are often those with the lowest incomes. Now, in these competitive times, who can be certain that a competitor is not going to step in with lower prices and offer better benefits?

Being unwilling to see themselves labelled as 'third age persons', some 50+ deliberately avoid these specific offers. Perversely, there are even those who do not make use of them. Unsurprisingly, these people are the younger and richer. This kind of reaction is likely to increase with the arrival of the baby boomers.

Another fact that has emerged from focus groups conducted with the over 50s is that some of them even become distrustful of businesses that offer rather spectacular reductions. They have adequate funds and stick to the adage: 'The cheap is expensive'.

On its own, therefore, using cheaper offers is not enough to ensure the loyalty of this clientele. Other factors are required.

Give them added value

We must remember that we are dealing with consumers who have many years of experience. They know precisely what they want. A man who has bought ten cars during his life knows what he has the right to expect from a new vehicle. This is true in all fields.

Some basic requirements have become their criteria for choice.

Quality

The 50+ are aware of it, more so than any other age group. They have suffered too much from the early offerings of the consumer society and its excesses. They know what a big brand can offer and are generally ready to pay the difference between a bad product and a quality one. In a 1996 survey of 522 over 50s carried out by Senioragency, quality was the first consideration before purchase for 89% of those questioned.

Let us quote a survey made in Germany about this element, a very interesting one as it compares different age groups in relation to quality and price.

The survey asked those interviewed to approve the comment that 'quality is more fundamental than the price of the product or service'. The percentage of people answering 'yes' is shown in Table 8.5.

Table 8.5 Quality more important than price

Age	Percentage of approval
Under 29 years	29
30–39 years	34
40–49 years	34
50–59 years	38
60–69 years	39
70 years and over	50
Source: GFK Marktforschung 1997	

Table 8.6 Confidence in brands and products			
	Total over 50s %	**50–59 years** %	**60–74 years** %	**75 years and over** %
French	82	72	86	90
Made in France	74	68	74	83
American	54	60	52	49
European	60.5	64	62	52
Japanese	53	60	50	47
Other Asian countries	34.7	42	30	32

Source: Senioragency

Durability

Just because one is over 50 is no reason to buy dubious products. Quite the contrary, one is confident and firmly intends to make full use of the products one acquires.

Another Senioragency study, involving 357 French over 50s, corroborates these two requirements of quality and durability. Are the over 50s aware of French-made or imported products? The figures in Table 8.6 show the 'patriotism' of the over 50s.

The Boulanger electrical goods chain in France took advantage of this phenomenon in 1996 when it launched its big promotion of French-made products and thereby attracted an over 50s clientele with good purchasing power.

The earlier Senioragency survey had posed the question: 'What are the most important criteria for you when you buy something?' The replies were as follows:

- 68% – I want it to last a long time

- 65% – I want it to be easy to use

- 59% – I want it to be really useful

- 57% – I want a guarantee and quality after-sales service.

Comfort

The older one gets, the more one looks for comfort. We want to feel good, surrounded by objects and services that make life more agreeable (and, we have the financial means to achieve this). From the pair of scissors specially designed for older hands, to the armchair that one can easily rise from, to the quiet and well lit restaurant, to the car that one can get out of without bending double. A large survey of over 50s (4000 people) in the Parisian area, carried out by the RATP, showed that the first requirement of this age group was greater comfort in the buses, trains and stations. There was also the request for the metro maps to be clearer and more readable (RATP responded to this with their 'Comfort plan'.)

Mail-order and telephone ordering companies also took this on board by developing appropriate catalogues, such as *Comfortably Yours* in the USA, and *Atout Confort* and *Confortis* in France.

Physical and financial security

The fear of being attacked, of falling and not being able to get up, of being ill, is a preoccupation of the over 50s. The world is not really a safe place and one cannot watch the TV news or read a daily paper without feeling vulnerable to daily attack.

Their major preoccupations are security for their health, well being and finance. The products and services that reassure them are those for the home (alarms, locks, other protective systems, emergency radio alarms). They also pay attention to those institutions that advise on insurance and financial investments. The wealth that they have accumulated during a lifetime of work is too precious to be put at risk.

Reassurance is the leitmotif of any discussion of whatever product or service that you wish to market. You must explain to the 50+ who you are, what it is that makes your product timeless and perennial, demonstrate the effectiveness of your product, and provide every detail that will help to remove any anxiety about a decision to buy. Do not hesitate to stress the backup assistance that they will be able to enjoy. Assistance is a magic word for them. Here we can quote the conclusions from the very large survey undertaken by Bengal Consulting in Scandinavia in the Spring of 2001, called 'Report on Scandinavian Seniors':

In many ways, this segment can be described as the ultimate rational consumers in the sense that they believe that the most important thing that can be communicated by an advertisement is the functionality of the product. Therefore, there appears to be a widespread need for rationalisation after the fact.

Succeed in ensuring that everyone involved becomes an 'ambassador' to the 50+

This is undoubtedly the key to success, but it is the most difficult to achieve. All the efforts of a business focused on winning over the 50+ may come to nothing if the customer service or sales force have not been trained to welcome, listen to and advise the over 50s.

For this target market, the quality of the relationship with company representatives is particularly important.

The over 50s detest the impersonal, cold and anonymous attitude that is in fashion. We should not forget that they include many who were born before the development of self-service, do-it-yourself and supermarkets. Their natural tendency is to seek out commercial contact, dialogue and individual advice.

Now, in our agitated age, counter-assistants and cashiers are rarely available. There are no longer any support staff and a given assistant is expected to do the work that would be shared between two or three staff some years ago. When an older man or woman approach with their questions (they have not immediately understood how to fill in such and such a form, or are taking time to make their choice), the assistant becomes irritated and agitated, and curses this 'old man' who is wasting his valuable time. Such a scenario is common in a number of shops, banks and other commercial outlets.

The lack of patience, attention and civility among sales and reception staff is the prime reason for the non-purchase of a product or service on the part of the over 50s. And this comes well above any question of cost. Here, as elsewhere, all retail managers would do well to take note. The Simm survey (12,000 interviews), carried out in France every two years using a very large sample, has highlighted the importance that the 50+ attach to reception, advice and service:

'I am ready to pay more if I am served well'

Base	under 50 years	over 50 years
100	86	136

'I want advice and service above all'

Base	under 50 years	over 50 years
100	81	133

This is why the American retail chains have embarked on vast training programmes for staff who come into contact with over 50s customers. The range extends from a new post called the 'greeter', held by an over 50-year-old, who welcomes all customers with a smile and a friendly word (Wal-Mart ran a good TV commercial on the topic), to a smaller trolley especially for the over 50s and packing of their purchases in convenient bags. They also created rest areas with refreshments, and staff to accompany customers to their cars with their purchases and help them to load them.

Other American businesses, banks, insurance companies and hotel chains, train their staff using videos. In France, Avis trained the staff at their 550 branches by distributing a videocassette called 'The 50+: a great opportunity for Avis', in advance of their launch of the Avis Club Senior card. In this cassette, management gave much practical advice on how to greet and advise customers of over 55. Other businesses have adopted the same approach to train their networks of agents and insurance brokers.

One piece of advice holds for all: select people of a similar generation to deal with the over 50s.

Conversation is immediately easier and advice is listened to, when it passes between two close age groups. There again, are older sales people not better because they are credited with experience and a wider knowledge of their trade than that of younger employees? Again, we refer to the UK retail chain B&Q, which in 1998 started to recruit over 50s for its stores. Today, about 13% of their 22,000 employees are aged over 50. There is lower absenteeism among these employees (39% lower than among younger employees), and they have an obvious empathy with customers. In Denmark, the DIY chain Silvan is also a pioneer in the field. 'In our satisfaction surveys, our customers, who tend to be in their 50s, ask for salespeople of their own age, who have sufficient experience to be able to advise them', according to Annette Schlünzen, director of human relations. The company embarked on a campaign to recruit older people and took on 30 salespeople of over 50. Following the success of this policy with customers, they now plan to aim for 25% of older people in each store. This said, many studies have proved that in the very technical areas (computers, photography) the 50+ prefer younger salespeople who are believed to be more capable of explaining new technology to them.

Show them consideration – roll out the red carpet

After working, economising, investing in their homes, educating their children, calculating and verifying, they have the right to enjoy themselves, breathe a little and generally take advantage of their situation.

This leads on to long-held dreams: beautiful holidays, the best restaurants and hotels, well-equipped cars, cruises and the big brands.

They have money and expect to be treated well. Retailers that offer home delivery are of interest: comfort, and the satisfaction of being served at home are legitimate pleasures. In France, there is the Télémarket telephone ordering service, minitel and since March 1998 operating via the Internet; the home delivery service introduced by the Monoprix supermarket chain has already more than 33% of its clientele aged over 50. Their loyalty can be consolidated by making them feel that they are privileged customers.

Adapt your conversation to their education level

Those working in marketing, promotion and advertising, whether with clients or agencies, have all achieved a high level of education (several years at university or business school after their secondary education). They are well able to manipulate the concepts and language of their advertising campaigns and direct marketing promotions and brochures. However, they all too frequently forget to adapt their language for consumers who may not have either their level of conceptualisation and understanding, or their vocabulary. This is true for all sectors of the population, but it is even more important to be aware of this when appealing to the over 50s. It should never be forgotten that the vast majority of current older pensioners, in all countries, do not have a level of education beyond that achieved up to the age of 12, 14 or 16. For them it was normal to start work young in order to help the family or leave home. Studies have shown that throughout the twentieth century children have received on average two to three years more schooling than their parents. (On the scale of a century this can turn out to be eight to ten more years for the young people of today compared with those of 1900.) If we consider the case of France, secondary school education ends at around the age of 18 with the passing of the baccalaureate examination (the equivalent of 'A' levels). In July 2001, the percentage of those passing (from the total of the 18-year-old generation) was 61.6%. Ten years earlier (1991), the figure was only 47.5%.

Table 8.7 Percentage of those gaining their baccalaureate* in France	
Examination year	**Percentage of generation members**
1906	1.1
1930	2
1940	3
1945	4.4
1955	5.3
1965	12.5
1970	20.5
1975	24.2
1985	29.4
1990	43.5
1995	62.7
2001	61.6

* Baccalaureate marks the end of school education, prior to moving on to further education at university, college and so on

Source: French Ministry of Education

When communicating with the over 50s, it should not be forgotten that 85% of them do not have A-levels (or equivalent qualification) (Table 8.7); if the target is the over 65s, the figure rises to 95%. In order to have a good chance of effectively communicating with them, it is essential to adopt a clear, simple language in tune with their vocabulary and level of comprehension.

Inform them, and inform them again

The 50+ are mad about information. They devour leaflets, brochures and catalogues. At any fair of exhibition you will see them besieging the stands to listen, ask questions and gather up the literature. Once back at their homes, they will have brought with them kilos of brochures and descriptions that they will work their way through before making an eventual purchase.

A spectacular initiative, called the '50+ Train' ('Le train des seniors'), took place in November 1996. Organised by Senioragency and the French

Railways (SNCF), it demonstrated this immense appetite for information. During the 12 days of its stops at the largest towns and cities of France, this exhibition train with five carriages and 14 different businesses represented had some 35,000 over 50s visitors, who were keen to investigate the products and services specifically created for them by these companies. The Zenith 'Exhibition for the active over 50s', held in Brussels, is on the way to becoming the largest European show of its kind. In December 2001, more than 30,000 visitors came to meet the 150 exhibiting organisations.

Time does not count for the 50+ as it does for those working. If necessary, they will not hesitate to spend several days comparing, visiting and being shown different products or services, not forgetting surfing the Internet for brands of interest and visiting sites to compare prices. With age, they have become less impulsive, wiser and more circumspect about what they are being offered. This is why there should be no exaggeration about the performance of a product or service. They are not to be hurried or driven to make an immediate decision; they have all their life before them. They are the true 'consumerists'.

Changes in the key senses: sight, hearing, touch, and their implications for marketing

Design for the young and you exclude the old. Design for the old and you include everybody.

It is not easy to put oneself in someone else's shoes, especially if this person is older than you are. The individual alone experiences such internal changes. Furthermore, the changes are slow and are spread out over decades. Identifying them helps to understand their implications for marketing to the over 50s.

It is difficult to determine precisely at what age the different phenomena of deterioration come to be more pronounced; it depends on the individual. As David Lebreton has written:

> Ageing is a slow and imperceptive process. A person moves gently from one day to the next, from one week to the next, from one year to the next; the events of daily life punctuate the flow of the day, not the awareness of time ... wear builds up on the face, enters the tissues, weakens the muscles, reduces energy, but without trauma, without sudden rupture ... the ageing process advances at walking pace.

Nonetheless, one can claim that the age of 50 is a significant marker throughout the world.

Sight

Eyesight declines from one's youngest years. It reaches its maximum capacity before the age of ten. From then on it declines. After 40, the crystalline lens tends to yellow and harden while the pupil contracts; opening and closing becomes slower. This contraction requires more external light (two to three times more than that required by adolescents). From the age of 50, it is said that nearly 90% of people require spectacles (for long-sightedness or presbyopia). Essilor realised before all its competitors the huge potential market for presbyopians and has successfully marketed its progressive Varilux lenses worldwide (see visual). The more one ages, the more serious the problems become.

VISUAL: Essilor has become number one in the world with its Varilux lenses designed for the enormous market of the presbyopes

Difficulty in distinguishing certain colours

Colours, such as blue, green, pink and violet, become difficult to identify. All pastel shades merge into a uniform halo. Mixtures of dark colours and pale colours are scarcely perceptible.

Practical implications for marketing

To overcome these problems, contrast must be used in visual items of communication destined for the over 50s. This ranges from the choice of colours and materials for an architectural interior to the colour codes for packaging.

In TV advertising spots, advertising posters and direct marketing mailings, foregrounds and backgrounds must be sufficiently contrasted and the use of red against blue avoided in order to prevent a monochrome effect on the part of the viewer. On packaging, reflective and shiny surfaces should be avoided.

Difficulty in adapting to sudden changes

Moving suddenly from darkness to light, and vice versa, or from one colour to another destabilises the vision. It then takes some time for the eye to readjust to seeing clearly again. Changing images incessantly runs the risk of causing visual chaos.

Practical implications for marketing

Reject completely in TV commercials the MTV clip video style of 15 shots in five seconds.

Go for longer shots, a more linear approach and long formats (such as for example 'infomercials' lasting one to two minutes screened during day-time schedules). It will be hard to adopt these common-sense principles because the designers and producers of advertising films are strongly influenced by the style of the big film-makers and the video clip culture. They find it hard to resist the ultra rapid style of a Goude or a de Mondino.

Loss in close-up vision

It becomes more and more difficult for the eye to see things that are close. An adolescent sees an object at 10 cm; a person of 70 sees it at 100 cm. It is estimated that only 15% of people over 75 have 10 by 10 vision.

After 50, one is usually unable to read fine print at less than 30–35 cm from the eye. The average visual accommodation faculty is:

14 diopters	at 10 years	2.5 diopters	at 50 years
10 diopters	at 20 years	1 diopter	at 60 years
4.5 diopters	at 40 years	0.25 diopter	at 70 years

Presbyopia arises from the change in the accommodation faculty of the crystalline lens. The eye refuses to focus its lens on close letters or objects. Spectacles become essential then, and unless adequate (such as those with progressive lenses), they often become insufficient. One then has to turn to the magnifying glass seen beside the telephone book or TV guide in the homes of the elderly.

Practical implications for marketing

Use a type body size larger than normal; 10 point is the minimum, with something between 12 and 14 point the ideal.

In addition, some typographic fonts are more difficult to read than others. Try to avoid fonts that are too complex or unusual and choose styles such as Times, Garamond or Century, with good inter-linear spacing for legibility.

Examples of fonts and sizes to be avoided:

This is Brush Script MT in 7pt

This is 8pt Lydian Csv BT

This is 9pt Lucida HBT

Examples of recommended font and sizes:

This is 11pt Times

This is 12pt Palatino

This is 13pt Arial

VISUAL: Audika is the number one chain in France for the distribution of hearing aids; through their ads they help to break down prejudice against the target group

Hearing

For those of us working in marketing and advertising, hearing is as important as sight.

Hearing deteriorates less perceptibly, and is therefore a more pernicious problem. It is estimated that about 33% of people aged over 60 have hearing problems. Recent studies show that 50% of the population never have their hearing tested and 47% of cases of deafness identified are neither corrected nor treated (survey made in 2000 by Audika in France). Largely for psychological reasons (because it shows), people are reluctant to wear a hearing aid. Some brands have embarked on persuading the public to overcome this complex, in particular the large players in the field, such as Phonak (Switzerland), Siemens (Germany), Starkey (USA), Danavox (Denmark). The most widespread hearing problems involve a loss of the high frequencies (called presbyacousia). This leads to a general merging of sounds and difficulty in separating them. People tend to talk more loudly to someone who is hard of hearing, but this does not help much since it is not a question of the volume but the pitch.

Practical implications for marketing

Create TV and radio spots with voices whose pitch compensates for the loss of high frequencies and scripts that are not too full so that the delivery is quiet and the articulation clear. Go for action where the players face the camera to facilitate lip reading. Lengthen the spot formats. Sounds should be clearly separated to avoid any confusion between voices, music and sound effects.

Touch

Arthritis and osteoarthritis strike quickly and hard. Half the people of 65 and over suffer from it, especially in the fingers. The result is that the oldest of the group have great difficulty in using their fingers. While this was unpleasant enough 30 to 40 years ago, this handicap is becoming intolerable, given the countless wrappings, packagings, blister packs, bottles, plastic films, safety caps, capsules, remote controls with tiny buttons and keys of ticket machines that we have to deal with. Consumer products are designed by young people for those who have full control of their hands.

There is no doubt that the USA has led the way in creating the awareness on the part of companies that most of our everyday products need to be redesigned (see visual). Medicines to relieve the problems of osteoarthritis and arthritis are a good example by making people aware of the pain and difficulty of those who suffer from these diseases. Advil has produced excellent ads on this topic.

Implications for marketing

There is an urgent need for proper design for the 50+. Product designers should bear in mind two keywords that will help achieve lasting success in an ageing society:

VISUALS: Advil has produced these brilliant ads to express the feelings and pain of people sufferering from athritis and osteoarthritis

Simplicity and user-friendliness

- Easy opening
- No redundancy
- Light to carry
- Ergonomics for objects
- Easy handling
- Friendly electronics

We will mention the initiative taken by British Gas in the UK with their programme called 'Through other Eyes'. All over the UK, British Gas employees have been wearing goggles, earplugs, rubber gloves and weights on their arms and legs to enable them to understand what it means to be one of their older customers. It is a way of making them age temporarily and leads to fundamental changes in thinking about shop floor design and the quality and relevance of service provided for older customers. 'This initiative has helped us realise that if we get it right for older people, we get it right for everyone,' says Val Mullany, PR manager. This is an approach similar to Ford's 'Third Age Suit', or the 'Age Simulator' utilised by several German industrial firms such as BSH Siemens-Bosch to make their new products suitable for an ageing population.

Advertising – the recipes that work

The over 50s are like nitroglycerine – to be handled with care. (Christophe Wilmart)

It is not easy to communicate with the 50+. They are demanding consumers, given to scepticism and not likely to be deceived by tricks.

The main difficulty for the advertising community is that for decades it has put all its knowledge and effort into serving the young. For the majority of those working in advertising agencies, the aim was to create a young image, a young style for the brands they were promoting, in a way that was sometimes exaggerated, obsessional even, in order to appeal to the millions of baby boomers and their children.

Huge effort was put into image makeovers, often at the clients' own instigation. Brands and company logos were redesigned, as were the premises. Packaging styles were altered in order to bring them into fashion. A young look was the order of the day.

For this to be achieved, control and decision-making was obviously put in the hands of young creative staff (35 is already an advanced age in many creative departments) who lived in a world of young people and who therefore 'felt' the music, films, fashions and trends that chimed with that age group. This was a perfectly justifiable choice in a demographically young society or one that was becoming younger.

But this is no longer true of all the large developed countries. Our consumers are ageing, and people have not prepared themselves to communicate with them. The advertising agencies must therefore be pushed into turning their attention to these dominant consumers in Europe. Such a revolution will not take place overnight and will face much hostility and scepticism. People are not going to easily give up what they have believed in and produced for so long. Moreover, as we have seen, the over 50s are saddled with the burden of negative images and preconceptions that are hard to dispel.

The aim of what follows is to draw up a list of the recipes and rules that are effective with the over 50s. First, we will draw everyone's attention to the need for prudence when interpreting this advice. There is no question of blindly following it or believing that it is bound to lead to success. We simply insist on the necessity of involving the 50+ in any pre-promotional testing for, with their sensitivity to language and pictures, they will quickly detect anything offensive that might be dismissed as unimportant by a professional without specialist experience of marketing to the over 50s. They will also be able to recognise any features of a proposed campaign that do not take into account the generation codes that are theirs. Consider, for example, this remark by a Swedish woman of 50, interviewed by Bengal Consulting:

> I think that sometimes you just don't understand what it is they are advertising. They show beautiful young people going somewhere, and then at the end of the advert you see the word Levi's, or something else, which you haven't been thinking about.

First piece of advice: be positive!

To make yourself understood, be positive! Any message addressed to the 50+ should not remind them about their problems. They are well aware of them. Focus rather on other things. They like life, want to enjoy it and are interested in everything; your product or service can be part of it. If your advertisement can simultaneously make them laugh and please them, then it is a success.

Your advertisement should show them achieving something new and exciting, taking on an ambitious project or helping others. Never forget that situations where their own sense of humour is shown to be triumphant are especially effective.

A successful example of this first point is the McDonald's TV spot, called 'The new kid' (see visual). First run in 1987, it was aimed at American over 50s and has rarely been surpassed in its portrayal of this age group.

McDonald's had become aware of some shortcomings in its ambience as far as the 50+ were concerned at a time when there was already much talk of the ageing of the American population. At the same time, theories on marketing to this age group were beginning to be listened to by some businesses.

VISUAL: 'The new kid' at McDonald's. One of the five
most liked TV commercials in the USA

McDonald's therefore undertook to embark on a very ambitious plan to win over the over-50s clientele by changing the interior decoration of its restaurants (more numerous and more comfortable seats, soft colours, and so on). New dishes, more suited to the diet requirements of this group were introduced and – a brilliant idea – they took on 50+ as employees.

A success at all levels, 'The new kid' TV spot is one of the five advertising commercials most liked by Americans ever.

The scenario is as follows: an oldish man leaves his home. In the street two friends going fishing call him and ask him to join them. 'I can't, I'm going to work', he replies to their astonishment. Cut to two young women servers in a McDonald's. One tells the other that they are getting a new male server that day, and the other says 'I hope he's cute …'. The grandfather arrives at the locked door of the restaurant. After signalling to him that he is too early for breakfast, the young woman realises that he is the 'new kid', and gently laughs at her mistake. The apprenticeship begins and the new server demonstrates such skills that his colleague asks in amazement 'Are you sure you've never done this before?' Come evening, the new kid returns home smiling. He tells his welcoming wife that he cannot understand how the restaurant has been able to manage without him up to now. This includes all the right ingredients to win over the over 50s: new experience, complicity between the young and the old, civility, satisfaction.

Second piece of advice: select a means of expression that sits halfway between advertising and information – the 'infomercial'

The older consumer is a somewhat prickly person who is much more wary of advertisers' arguments than the younger consumer. Such a consumer is only moderately impressed by the vast majority of advertisements which appear to favour style over content and are basically aimed at a young public ('commercials made by the young for the young'). Several surveys have revealed this division between the over 50s and the majority of TV commercials.

In February 1997, IFOP carried out a survey of 502 people over 60 in France. Their opinion of TV commercials was damning. 'TV advertising – irritates: 73%; entertains: 13%; interests: 6%; no stated preference; no opinion: 8%.'

Another survey had already identified this dissatisfaction. Senioragency conducted a survey in France, Belgium and Holland among individuals over 50 that included the following two questions: 'Do you have the feeling that in general TV commercials are intended for you?' The reply to this was no: 61%, yes: 39%. In response to the complementary question 'If not, what criticisms would you make of those TV commercials that you know?', 72% said that the TV spots were too complicated and sometimes bizarre; 60% said that they were only aimed at young people, and 43% said that the message was not clear.

In Germany, Grey strategic planning department carried out several surveys in 1998 among 50+ customers to identify their criticisms of advertising in general. Their comments are very clear:

■ 'In advertising they only show young people', for 63% of 50+

■ 'In advertising they seldom show seniors', for 46% of 50+

■ 'In advertising seniors are never represented as they really are', for 51% of 50+

■ 'In advertising seniors are not presented seriously and are depicted in a disrespectful way', for 31% of 50+.

A hasty conclusion about these surveys would fall back on the so-called advertising phobia of the over 50s. In fact, it is not the advertising that the 50+ do not appreciate, it is rather a certain dominant style of advertising, the 'unique advertising idea', that is the cause. That is, a production on the grand scale that as a matter of course contains aesthetics, humour, tricks, puns; in other words more emphasis on style than content, without forgetting the forever young, beautiful and fit actors and actresses, with whom it is scarcely possible to identify (can one really be expected to identify with someone who is probably 40 years younger?). They have had enough of these TV spots, if only because of problems of sight and hearing, not to mention their aggressive, visually jumpy images and saturated colours, delivering skimpy information at high speed, just like other clip videos. Here, we can quote another person interviewed by Bengal Consulting in Norway, a 50-year-old man who said:

> I think the adverts say so little. They say nothing about the product's authenticity and quality, it's just a brand. I want more facts in adverts.

There is a solution to winning over and reassuring the 50+; this is the 'infomercial', an American neologism from 'information' and 'commercial'. This type of advertisement has developed strongly in the USA over the past 15 years with the rapid growth of cable and local TV. With vast amounts of airtime to fill that the big national advertisers were not interested in, these stations were happy to find companies ready to produce long messages (sometimes up to 28 minutes!) promoting a product and with a green number allowing the viewer to order the product immediately. In the beginning, attention was focused on 'second level' products, but following popular success, all the big brands gradually moved over to the infomercial. Today, it is estimated that nearly 10% of US TV advertising adopts this format.

In many other countries it is, at present, impossible to screen advertising messages of such length, owing to legislation, advertising congestion and the hostility of TV journalists. The compromise has been the introduction of a European-style infomercial, as in France where spots lasting from one to three minutes have been screened since 1996. Senioragency has specialised in these throughout Europe. We shall examine why it is that the new type of advertising constitutes one of the most effective means of communicating with the over 50s. In fact, without exception, in all countries the 50+ are the largest population of TV viewers. Since they have much more free time than those who are working, they tend to watch the broadcast programmes of the national or large company networks. On average they watch 30 to 40% more TV than those under 50.

■ The 50+ consumer, being prudent, suspicious even, needs much more information before deciding to buy. Because of its unusual length, the infomercial is able to deliver a large number of facts and arguments about the product

■ Through its scenario, the infomercial can tackle the obstacles to purchase (for example, through dialogue) and reply point by point to any objections (see visual)

■ By showing a freephone number during part or the whole of the spot, it facilitates direct interactive contact to provide further information or to place an order

■ By far the most persuasive factor for the over 50s is that, for many of them, the infomercial is not advertising. In fact, the simplicity of the technical presentation, the matter-of-fact style and the focusing of the discussion on the product are totally different from other advertising spots. The 50+ viewer appreciates the absence of superfluous decoration and devours the infomercial like a marketing videocassette or like an advertising press editorial on TV

■ Finally, in order to be effective and economically viable, this type of advertising spot is screened during the daytime, that is between 6.00 and 17.00–18.00 during the week, and during direct marketing periods

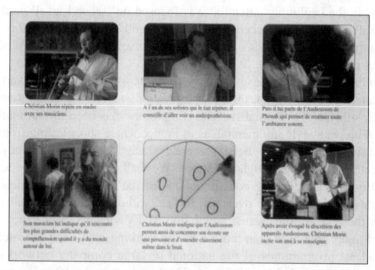

VISUAL: Example of an infomercial for the over 50s. The problem is outlined and then the advantages of the product are explained point by point, terminating with an invitation to telephone in

Source: Audio Zoom by PHONAK

when the 50+ are particularly receptive. Moreover, many of them watch TV with a notepad, pencil and telephone within reach. On the other hand, if the same advertisement were to be screened in prime time, when the 50+ are watching the news or a film, it would provoke virtually no response, because they regard any advertising put out at that time as 'pollution'. Utilising these off-peak periods has the great advantage of allowing the advertisers to enjoy extremely attractive rates (only a few hundred euros for the most economical). In this way brands can be presented for long periods for budgets that cost 5 to 6 times less than those required to reach the under 50s.

To illustrate this new type of advertising, we will take the example of the infomercial for the Phonak range of hearing aids (one of the largest world brands distributed in France). Filmed by Pascal Thomas and lasting for 1.3 minutes, it portrays a group of musicians rehearsing with the well-known French clarinettist, Christian Morin. This film allows the company to explain how its AudioZoom system works in a very detailed and instructive way (using a paperboard); something that would have been totally impossible with a classic advertising format. With the green number free call number shown for a full minute, the viewer can call to ask for complete documentation on the device and the addresses of local hearing centres.

Third piece of advice: feature advertising celebrities of their generation

The basic aim of advertising is to make brands stand out in an advertising environment that grows increasingly crowded.

When considering the over 50s, the situation becomes even more complex, because the vast majority of spots are not at all designed to interest them. All the more reason why they resent them. It is therefore essential to find some simple means of attracting their attention and making them understand that message being transmitted is specifically directed towards them.

Each generation produces its own heroes, stars and personalities who can arouse interest and sympathy. One of the formulas that functions internationally with the 50+ is to feature celebrities who are known to their generation in advertisements. The enormous advantage of this approach is that at the precise moment when this person appears on the screen, the 50+

viewers understand that this advertisement is aimed at them. Another advantage is the guarantee for the product or service that this person brings; remembering that the 50+ are more suspicious than other consumers, the fact that a personality whom they admire has taken the risk of being associated with such a brand is immediately taken to be a pledge of sincerity. The presence of a mediator standing alongside a brand imbues it with the status of great brand or 'great subject', for example Bob Dole for ED (erectile dysfunction) in a TV advertising campaign for Pfizer in the USA.

Of course, featuring a person known to the members of a generation acts as a strong boost to the awareness of the brand among the target market. This is very useful in these times of intense competition between brands and provides a mathematical competitive advantage; it engenders psychological closeness and 'top of the mind' awareness which hasten spontaneous response. The choice of the celebrity is of course crucial. Each person must be examined according to his or her personality and conduct to ensure compatibility with the type of product or service. Then, the scenario must be built around that person so that he or she appears as natural as possible (there is nothing worse than to have someone act a role that is not credible).

Finally, avoid featuring people who are out to secure the limelight at all costs; there is nothing worse than those 'stars' who one sees one day drinking a beer, another day eating a sausage, another day visiting the bank, and so on. The over 50s will see them as insincere and mercenary.

The famous French navigator, Eric Tabarly, a legend in the sailing world, was featured to launch Zuritel, the first direct car insurance scheme aimed exclusively at pensioners over 60 (see visual). Eric was a spirited pensioner of 67, and a symbol of security (essential for an insurance company). He never wasted words (something that was an implicit way of showing the importance of this revolution in the insurance industry as it emerged from its legendary silence). He had also never lent his name to another brand. The gains in awareness of Zuritel testify to the effectiveness of bringing together these two images. Launched in June, 1996, with zero awareness, by February 1997 the brand had achieved 25% global awareness among its target market; this rose to 28% in May, 41% in September and 52% in December 1997. Within less than 18 months, Zuritel had caught up with the pioneer of direct car insurance in France, Eurofil (a subsidiary of the UK's Commercial Union), that had first appeared six years previously and had spent three times more on its launch.

VISUAL: Featuring the famous navigator, Eric Tabarly brought spectacular success to the launch of Zuritel's direct car insurance for the over 60s

Fourth piece of advice: surround them with people of other generations

Grandparents like to show kindness to their grandchildren and to teach them about life. In the best of situations, there is even total complicity between the two generations. The other advantage is that when the child becomes an adolescent he or she will share personal secrets and worries with grandparents in preference to parents.

It is therefore a great stage for people over 50; they have children, but none of the disadvantages of having children!

Who has not seen their father radically changed when becoming a grandfather? New patience, tolerance, greater availability – one has never known him like that!

For the 50+, the family has become the centre of happiness. Contact with young children and adolescents is a kind of rejuvenating bath that brings infinite pleasure.

Internationally, in the large developed countries, one person in two at the age of 56 has at least one grandchild. At the age of 70, 80% of that generation are grandparents or great grandparents. Currently, on average one becomes a grandmother at 50 and a grandfather at 52.5. On average, grandparents have four grandchildren (in the EU). This adds up to considerable numbers. For example, in 2001, there are nearly 14 million grandparents in the UK and 12.5 million in France. Every over 50s parent is a potential grandparent.

This is why, in advertising commercials, they especially appreciate those moments when they see themselves surrounded by young people, because these moments create harmony between the generations. Advertising can portray this harmony.

Some successful commercials have played upon this emotional theme. We can mention Werther's Original sweets whose advertisement shows a

VISUAL: Azzaro has created a very original 'inter-generational' image

typical grandfather and his grandson, or the very original poster and press ads for the Chrome de Azzaro perfume range that had the idea of showing three male generations, a less conventional way of pointing up the relationship between generations (see visual). In the field of charity, some advertisers have learnt how to exploit this sentiment (remember that the over 50s are the main donors) and a suffering child anywhere in the world is able to 'open the heart' of any grandparent.

Fifth piece of advice: portray them as they see themselves, lively and attractive

At a recent creative focus group meeting, when asked to provide a slogan that portrayed their image in the eyes of other sections of society, people over 50 came up with: 'Fit? I am, always!'

This reveals the perception they have of themselves – a perception that is often correct. They expect advertising to honour this vision of themselves, in particular so that it will help to banish for good those negative preconceptions that they are saddled with.

Since they are fit, we should show them as active, lively and the driving force in situations that show the value of their punch and dynamism.

A talented American commercial for the Nike brand shows a baseball team whose average age is 76; the star of the spot is aged 100. This commercial is powerful and credible because it is based on an authentic case, making everyone want to be like this man at his age. The finale of the film is spectacularly successful. The star says 'It must have been the shoes!' The spot ends with the brand's marvellous slogan 'Just do it!', a perfect message to bridge the generations.

The Unilever Group screened in Europe a very effective and amusing commercial for its Olivio spread brand depicting some over 60s men playing football and at the same time gently flirting with their spectator wives. The Fruit d'or oil version that appeared in France on TV and in the over 50s press was based on the same theme (see visual).

Another very successful advertisement was launched world-wide in the autumn of 2000 by Estée Lauder, the giant American beauty products corporation, to promote its face cream for the more mature woman. For Resilience Lift, the brand had the idea of once again featuring its star model of the 1970s, Karen Graham, who was aged 23 when she had first appeared for them. Now, 30 years later, she was asked to perform again. Better still, since Karen Graham had always been keen on fly-fishing (sic!) and had, at the end of her modelling career, opened a fishing school in

Quel âge donneriez-
vous à cette bande de
jeunes d'une soixantaine
d'années?

Fruit d'or
C'EST BON MAINTENANT
ET POUR PLUS TARD.

VISUAL: Fruit d'or asks the 'age' of those young boys
in their 60s; a talented, humorous approach

Montana, the advertiser had the excellent idea of having her adopt the same pose as 30 years previously, dressed in a fishing outfit (see visuals).

This was a striking parallel and an especially brilliant and convincing demonstration that a woman can be as beautiful and attractive in her 50s. It gave a very fine message of hope to all women at, or approaching, this age.

Sixth piece of advice: tell them about the product, they are only interested in that

'Tell me about myself, that's all I am interested in', is one interpretation. In this case, the 50+ would tend rather to expect an advertising campaign to do its job of conveying information on the promised product and service before embellishing them.

For them, the star is the product, the tangible reality, argued and verifiable. Commercials or spots that give the impression of favouring appearance and aesthetics over content rarely move them. They want the concrete; they want to have it explained to them why this product should be tried, and perhaps chosen, from the rest.

VISUALS: The same lady for Estee Lauder, with 30 years between the two ads: eternal youth and beauty, a very convincing message

They are not inclined to swing suddenly towards some new offer without a reason.

Creative staff at advertising agencies are often told that they should not bore readers of their advertisements with too much body copy, since the average time spent reading an advertisement is only a few seconds. Only 3% of consumers read all the body copy. Let us cancel these instructions and make them work in the opposite direction; the over 50s want to know everything about the product and service.

50+ Marketing

An effective way of communicating with them is to use the magazine press or direct marketing mailings. We should not forget that they belong to the generation of the written word, which is the only medium for developing an argument in detail. This is why the press infomercial (see visuals) is a really appropriate technique for capturing their attention and giving them enough information to dispel their concerns and show them the

VISUALS: Examples of press infomercials – an emblematic over 50-year-old and a detailed argument with humour

sincerity of the offer and the business behind it. One cannot overstress the fact that they belong to the generation that invented consumerism (Ralph Nader is aged 65). They need to know *everything* before deciding to buy.

Seventh piece of advice: Hello, who's speaking?

The 50+ love to talk, be listened to and ask questions; they are consumers who like conversation, which is good news for the brands. As we have seen, they have time, and need to verify and compare before making their choice. They are prime candidates to conduct a quality discussion with businesses. Advertisers who favour the coupon approach will find them a happy hunting ground.

This is a target market that wants to go to the limit with the brands that communicate with it. It would therefore be a pity not to lace your message with one or more of the many interactive elements available today. The traditional cut-out coupon, of course, but also the freephone number and your Internet site address will facilitate contact between potential customers and your brand. They may well rush to their telephones on a huge scale after the screening of a good infomercial or direct marketing spot during the daytime. It is not rare to receive several hundred callers in the ten minutes that follow such a TV spot.

A word of caution though, once contact has been made, there must be no question of disappointing them with impatient call service operators and brief or unreadable information literature. They can then react very unfavourably and, without turning a hair, boycott companies that have wasted their time.

Eighth piece of advice: switch on to their wavelength

At the risk of appearing banal, one should recall one obvious fact. Who, better than an over 50-year-old, knows what interests them, and what can make them change their brand? No one, but themselves.

One of the basic rules of marketing is to go and find out the needs of one's potential consumers, however well or badly they can express them. Any work on marketing recommends the sampling of consumers before any new launch or promotion. We would thoroughly endorse this.

The vast majority of marketing managers who venture into the world of the 50+ have the wrong ideas about this market, which they do not understand properly. The 50+ market is neither monolithic, nor uniform. There is a gulf between a man of 55 still actively working and a man of 70, who has been retired for many years. This fact makes it necessary for advertising managers to segment this market carefully and think about the product offers that are made to it. Every idea for a product, service, form of packaging or promotional message must, without fail, be pre-tested among different segments of the over 50s market. Some reactions from groups of 50+ that reject the creative ideas and the product suggestions are surprising, even though these products seemed to embrace all the elements required for their approval. The answer is to verify and validate; and this, sooner rather than later.

Ninth piece of advice: think about the baby boomers

Since the beginning of 1996, the ageing curve of the population has made a spectacular climb owing to the post-war hordes of children now reaching the age of 50. These children are the result of an international demographic phenomenon, unprecedented in the history of humanity – the baby boom.

The origins are well known. Ecstatic at having survived the Second World War unscathed, young men and women of the time wanted to have families. This wave of births extended to all countries of the Western world.

These children of the baby boom witnessed the extraordinary emergence of the 'affluent society', which, from the 1960s to the 1990s, swept everyone along with it in a frenzy of over consumption. The baby boomers were the most enthusiastic players in this. They acquired the habit of being pleasure seekers above all; hence the US name the 'Me generation'.

They also became fervent 'believers' in their bodies. Well aware that this item of 'capital' was something that required much attention to make it more attractive (hence the huge growth in aesthetic and cosmetic surgery), they also kept it healthy (wholesome and balanced diet, no excess) in order to feel fit and well.

Turning 50 does not upset their lifestyle or way of thinking. They therefore apply themselves to perpetuating their lifestyle by making certain necessary adjustments in the face of family and physical requirements.

The arrival of the baby boomers will expand the 50+ market and add to their economic domination. These newcomers will have even more sophisticated demands as consumers and these ageing baby boomers are the current topic of interest in the USA. Dozens of articles appear about them throughout the economic press. The fact is that they represent no less than 78 million consumers in the USA alone.

Increasingly, one sees appearing products or commercials that play on nostalgic sentiment to remind the baby boomers of their youth, whether

VISUAL: New Beetle advertising clearly aimed
at 'ageing baby boomers'. What a talent!

consciously or unconsciously. The most symbolic example of this is, of course, the new Beetle, conceived and designed by Volkswagen for the affluent baby boomers. The advertising campaign makes brilliant use of the 'flower power' theme (see visual). We should mention too the skill of Chrysler's designers with the PT Cruiser or the new Mini from Rover. As the former CEO of Chrysler, Lee Iacocca said:

> Be watchful of your customers. You must follow them where they go. You must change when their lives change. I have followed the baby boomers throughout my career. I gave them wheels with the Ford Mustang in 1964. Twenty years later, when they had had their children, dogs and nannies, I offered them family models. Today, I am going to win them over with the electric bicycle. (Lee Iacocca, founder of Global Motors Inc, August 2001)

Summary of the over 50s' expectations of advertising

A survey carried out by Sofres is very interesting, because it enables a comparison to be made between the attitude of the over 50s and that of younger people (Table 8.8).

It is not surprising that the over 50s expect advertising to be above all clear and easily understood, which is not always the case.

As for humour, 25% of them expect an advertisement to be funny. But this percentage is well below the figures for the other age groups, especially those aged 25–34.

The most mediocre score relates to the fantasy question. This underlines their very concrete attitude towards communication.

	18–24 years %	25–34 years %	35–49 years %	50–64 years %	65 years and over %
Table 8.8 What are the most important things you expect from an advertisement?					
It should be clear and easy to understand	32	28	39	47	49
It should be funny	38	47	32	25	25
It should be creative	43	31	32	20	16
It should be beautiful	25	21	18	22	17
It should be surprising	26	20	14	11	7
It should make you fantasise	15	11	11	10	5

Source: Sofres, France

The 1996 Senioragency survey showed that the expectations of this market had become more refined. The three basic expectations were:

1. Advertising should be clear and understandable for 53% of them
2. Advertising should inform about new products for 42% of them
3. Advertising should give precise information about a product or service for 39% of them.

We should again refer to the very large survey carried out by Bengal Consultancy among Scandinavian over 50s in the Spring of 2001:

Information and relevancy appear to be important factors when it comes to getting this segment to regard advertising in a positive way.

We are definitely dealing with a very rational consumer!

The 50+ are very serious about advertising. They want to know all the details about a company, and the brand, products and services it tries to sell them. It is for them the first criteria of an efficient advertisement. When you have delivered sufficient 'objective' information, you can add some humour to please them. Always remember that we are targeting very experienced consumers who are never in a hurry to waste their money on bad products or poor services! They want to know *everything* about you before considering buying or ordering!

CHAPTER 9

Conclusion

Life before 50 is nothing but a warm up
(FAMOUS SLOGAN FROM AARP)

The wave of ageing continues to increase in size. In 2040, half of the European population will be aged over 50. This trend is the same in all the developed countries. It is time to prepare for this state of affairs and to put in place a fundamental cultural revolution.

Let's try to draw up a panorama of several great social, economic and psychological developments that we shall have to face up to.

The 15 opulent years

One could call them the 15 glorious years, because the next 15 years will mark the economic high point of the over 50s. Their prosperity will continue to increase as a result of two phenomena.

The first will be the replacement of the 75s and over, whose incomes are on the whole relatively modest, by the Masters and Liberated who are infinitely better provided for financially as they will benefit from the marvellous pension systems that were introduced from the beginning of the 1950s. The younger generations will be the ones to suffer from the new operating rules brought about by weaker financial conditions, not the older ones.

The second phenomenon, whose effects are already beginning to appear, is the arrival at retirement of women who have earned their own pensions from their salaried employment. Thirty-five years ago, the 'liberation' of women drove millions of them to leave their kitchens and take up a professional career. This second pension in the household will add considerably to the disposable income of retired couples and add to the financial clout of the 50+ in the income statistics. One can reckon on an improvement of around 50% in the income contributed by a second pension, after deducting new taxation that have been introduced to cut back on some of the advantages of the retired.

The next 15 years offer a tremendous marketing opportunity to businesses that are able to capture the interest of the over 50s.

> The increase in the economic influence of the over 50s is now written into our future; it can be claimed, with little chance of error, that they will exceed 50% of the social income towards the middle of the next decade and that, in 2020, they will have exceeded the 60% mark. (Credoc, March 1997)

The outlook for tomorrow is fine, but the day after tomorrow there is the danger that it will be less good for the millions of future pensioners, now aged 30, who must from now on accept pension systems that cannot be sustained.

Emergence of the 'sandwich generation'

The constant advance in life expectancy has an immediate and striking result in many families; it is not unusual for a child to know its great grandparents. The Swiss group, Novartis Phrama, carried out a survey to learn more about 'five-generation families', something that would have been an impossible task only a decade ago.

Increased lifespan will upset the balance in families. The pyramid system, with few old people and many children, will be transformed into a funnel-shaped system, with many old people at the top and few young people at the base.

At the family level, the 'sandwich generation' appears. It consists of men and women between 30 and 55 who, at the same time, have to help and assist the preceding generation and their own children (see Figure 9.1).

In certain cases, this responsibility may become overwhelming when the problems of health and dependency of the old are combined with lack of employment of the young (about a quarter of those aged 50–65 have a relation who is not independently self-sufficient).

This new sociological phenomenon threatens to become the fate of many baby boomers whose parents, today, enjoy good health. However, in the future, when their health declines, the situation will be different.

The French National Pensions Office (CNAV) published in November 1993 the results of a survey that was a 'world first'. With the assistance of

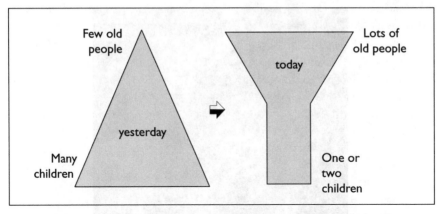

Figure 9.1 Configuration of yesterday's and today's family

Source: Senioragency

Insee, CNAV took a representative sample of people, born between 1939 and 1943, living in Paris and having at least one living parent and an adult child. Some 4668 people were interviewed, including nearly 1000 groups of three and 725 groups of two. The data across these three generations highlighted a phenomenon that CNAV described as the 'pivot generation', that is, those aged 49–53. This generation helps both its parents (80% of the sample) and its children (96%). This help takes many forms: help for dependent parents, car transportation, banking surety, upgrading domestic equipment, payment for education and, finally, gifts or loans of money to children (64%) and to parents (9%).

Looking after parents becomes all the more complicated, as modern life inexorably puts distance between family members. For example, in 1960 in the USA, 40% of those over 65 lived under the same roof with one of their adult children; by 1999, this figure had dropped to 4%.

It is most often the woman, the mother, the daughter, or the daughter-in-law, who finds herself surrounded on all sides, always called upon by her children, her parents or her parents-in-law. In terms of marketing, this consumer, who is also a recommender, has a determining role. Choosing a home or a retirement home is not only something done by the Peaceful, but also by their children. Remember that something recommended by an adult child has a high probability of being listened to. They and their generation, who know about TV, video recorders and PCs, merit the most trust, because they have learnt about and mastered these products and services.

There are famous examples of the successful marketing of third age retirement homes by American property developers who addressed their

VISUAL: AARP helps the members of the sandwich
generation to take care of their parents

message primarily to the children of aged parents (see visual). They
simply demonstrated the psychological and physical relief of having one's
parents in such medically supported institutions close to one's own home.
A TV advertising campaign screened in France, promoting the Résidence
St-Remy of the Orpea Group, illustrated this in a striking way. More than
70% of the responses were from people aged 50 to 65 speaking on behalf
of their fathers or mothers.

More or less everywhere in the world, new Internet sites are being
created to help the over 50s to find satisfactory answers to the health and
housing problems of their aged parents.

The young person – a 'disappearing species'

The future is frankly not rosy for young people in the coming years.
They will become increasingly isolated in the middle of a flood of silver-
haired people.

There is the danger that the capitalist world, because it is built entirely for the benefit of the all-powerful teenager, will quickly malfunction if it continues to target a population that grows more restricted all the time.

But what a cultural revolution we have in prospect!

It will not be easy to throw out the intricate marketing techniques developed to gain the attention of the young. Those brands that have invested huge sums in all kinds of promotion media in order to be fashionable, face the painful prospect of being called to account. Mass marketing has been based on the principle that there will always be more new consumers wanting to try new products.

This belief works perfectly when there are millions of young and enthusiastic consumers, ready to try anything because of their adventurous spirit.

What becomes of this system, when faced with tens of millions of informed and stringently demanding consumers who are not be fooled? These 50+ customers who are ready to buy, provided that what is on offer is a real improvement on the product or service that they already know. These people, who are not easily won over by arguments about 'style', when their first priority is 'content'.

The road will be bumpy for many brands and for their advertising agencies. At the social level, the task will be no easier. For decades, all community efforts have been directed towards children (nursery schools, sports facilities, swimming pools, universities, maternity hospitals, and so on) while the over 50s have more or less been forgotten. Here, too, it will be necessary to change direction and bring community priorities into line with demographic facts.

A final word

To all those, and I know there are many, who still doubt the necessity of taking an immediate interest in the extraordinary potential of the ageing population and allocating adequate marketing resources to it, I would simply say 'Open your eyes'.

Open your eyes and see how the 50+ in your circle live. Open your eyes at airports, at sports grounds and golf courses, in the theatre, concert hall and on TV; watch the most skilled craftsmen, artists, doctors ... I bet they are 50+!

I am sure you have understood that we are no longer in a 'youth world', so now 'Just do it!' and you will be able to expand your business in the years to come.

INDEX